Ben Selinger was Professor of Chemistry at the Australian National University in Canberra, and has been a visiting professor at universities in the USA, the UK, Canada, Israel, Germany and Thailand. However, he is not your average academic professor of Chemistry. He presented 'Dial a Scientist', a science talkback programme on ABC Radio, writes feature articles for the *Canberra Times* in addition to his fortnightly column, 'So why is it?', and is a winner of the Special Eureka Award for science communication. He has initiated and contributed to setting many national standards for consumer products and is again on the Council of the Australian Consumers Association, publisher of *Choice*. He is currently Senior Associate (Canberra) with Jackson Wells Morris Communications, dealing with Science and Technology Issues management.

Why
the
watermelon
won't ripen
in your armpit

and other science
conundrums

Why
the
watermelon
won't ripen
in your armpit

and other science
conundrums

BEN SELINGER

ALLEN & UNWIN

First published in 2000

Copyright ©Ben Selinger 2000

Allen & Unwin
9 Atchison Street
St Leonards NSW 2065 Australia
Phone: (61 2) 8425 0100
Fax: (61 2) 9906 2218
E-mail: frontdesk@allen-unwin.com.au
Web: http://www.allenandunwin.com

National Library of Australia
Cataloguing-in-Publications entry:

Selinger, Ben, 1939– .
  Why the watermelon won't ripen in your armpit and other
  science conundrums.

Includes index.
ISBN 1 86508 289 9.

  1. Science—Popular works. I. Title.

500

Set in 11/13 pt Janson Text by DOCUPRO, Sydney
Printed in Australia by McPherson's Printing Group

10 9 8 7 6 5 4 3 2

Foreword

A T THE DAWN of the new millennium, science affects us in a relentless and intimate way. The air we breathe, the food we eat, the way we travel, the animals we keep, the homes we live in, the deodorants and cosmetics we put on our bodies, and even the children we produce are all increasingly controlled by science.

This century will see babies born with improved genes. For instance, cancer genes or diabetes genes will be removed and replaced with healthy genes. This is the most wonderful time for science, but there are problems. Whilst science itself gets better and better, science communication remains an embarrassment. The scientific community often feels that science is a matter for scientists and that their job is not one of service to the general community. Those scientists who do understand that they, like everyone else, have the privilege of doing what the bulk of ordinary people require of them, still often lack the communication skills to reach out to non-scientists. This is where Ben Selinger comes in. His knowledge of science is impeccable and he tells a really good yarn. We need people like Ben right now because most of us are battling to understand even the basics of chemistry, genetics and human health.

It would be a very foolish world that left science entirely to scientists. Somehow we must all come up to speed in the basics of the science that affects us. Maybe we don't need to understand relativity or the finer points of the Big Bang theory, but we do need to understand the bits that land on our bodies, go into our mouths and shape our babies.

Sometimes science makes mistakes. We need to know what those mistakes are and what to do about them.

Science produced the organochlorine insecticides (the DDT family) and in a survey done some years ago, 98 per cent of Perth women produced breast milk contaminated by these chemicals. This is of great concern to us all. Ben Selinger is one of the heroes of science. It was he, as chairman of the National Registration Authority for Agricultural and Veterinary Chemicals in Australia, who finally removed the DDT family of chemicals from Australia forever.

This is not to say that science is evil. Overall science and scientists benefit society enormously. And science does not make many major mistakes. But increasing disillusionment with science has lead to alternative medicines now becoming more popular than those produced by mainstream science.

While many scientists continue to wear their white lab coats and diligently squirrel away behind their laboratory benches, people like Ben Selinger are reaching out to everyone, offering digestible pearls of scientific wisdom.

I earnestly commend this book to you all. I am proud to call Ben a friend and I'm grateful for the scientific knowledge that I have received from him.

This book covers many of the areas that most people need to know. And it does so with a light and often witty touch. So much for the turgid introduction—it gets better from here on, I promise.

Don Burke

Contents

Water

Metals

Cosmetics

In and out of the office

Out to dinner—all froth and bubbles

Serious stuff

Introduction

WHEN THE TIMES are tough and the road is long, it helps to remember what the Armenians say: 'The watermelon will not ripen in your armpit'. This is one of 18 500 proverbs collected in the Prentice Hall *Encyclopedia of World Proverbs* by folklorist and professor, Wolfgang Mieder. Being of similar mind to Professor Mieder I find this advice appropriate for science today. Science cannot afford to hide its light under a bushel; if it wants public support, it has to be seen, and seen to be useful. And if possible, fun! (Armpits are a major item for discussion in the section on deodorants where I consider everything from stopping the odours to extracting and using them as sex attractants.)

I have been contributing pieces to the *Canberra Times* for 25 years, and writing a regular column for the last two. Such pieces are fun to write and hopefully provide digestible chunks of useful information for the reader. As a writer, I have about three seconds in which to grab the reader, and about 500 words to hold her. And readers are not shy in phoning, faxing or e-mailing comment, correction, approval and disapproval. My minder, Simon Grose, who edits the science and technology sector in the *Canberra Times*, has made sure what is written is interesting, useful, intelligible and topical.

All this has helped me in writing this book, which has also provided me with a chance to revisit topics and to collate them logically. Those wanting to explore further will probably find more detail and technical background in my comprehensive book, *Chemistry in the Marketplace* (5th edition, 1998, Allen & Unwin).

About us

We are all involved in chemical warfare of one form or another, if only in our cupboards or in the garden, as the section on Health shows. There is no getting away from it, chemicals 'r' us. What implications does genetic engineering of foods have for our health? What is so bad about drugs? (The natural ones, on which we still depend, are magic—which is what they were first used for.) Is it possible to say NO to sex? (Not if NO stands for nitric oxide because we now 'know' this simple gas is responsible for erections.) Why have we almost lost the war on antibiotic resistance?

You probably know all there is to know about food, but do you know what makes eggs go green, or how a flash in the pan from a sizzling steak could save your life aboard a navy ship? The aroma of frying explains the global pollution form DDT and PCB and other nasties. Sick of eating tasteless starchy gassed bananas? That is not all that ethylene gas can do. Swallowing the latest elixir of anti-oxidant pills to enslave those 'free-radicals'? Read the full story. Vegetarians beware, the plants are out to get their revenge. Finish off the section on food with a good historical cup of coffee.

Learning new material is hard work. It is much easier to pick it up by osmosis. Osmosis is actually a very important concept, particularly if you like clean water. Or even if you just like throwing water over a curvaceous T-shirt, it could be most useful to have a scientific excuse. Read lots about water in the third section of the book.

Napoleon Bonaparte discovered that winters were the best time to lose trousers. On his way to Russia during a really cold winter campaign, his soldiers lost theirs. No, not by exposure to Russian maidens, but exposure to the extreme cold, which turned the tin used for buttons in the uniforms from a strong metal into a crumbling powder of non-metal. More details are to be found in the section on metals.

Armpits are a major resource for research. We need materials to stop them stinking and we extract their essence in our search for elusive female sexual attractants. So far, female goats and sows have been the major beneficiaries. Intrigued? Go to the section on cosmetics.

Most people wouldn't, but there are compelling reasons why someone might want to leave an opened unused condom on the office photocopier. It is quite a sensitive device and could save you from serious illness. Not from AIDS, but from ozone. Find out more in 'In and out of the office'.

There may be more to life than froth and bubbles, but that doesn't mean they aren't terribly interesting as 'Out to dinner' explains. And if you want more, you'll find the serious stuff in the final section.

Finally, if all this gets you down, remember the Australian discovery that the lightest metal of all, lithium, is great in treating some forms of depression. So is reading this book.

What really *is* science?

A EUROPEAN UNION survey in 1997 on public trust, asking who is telling the truth on genetically modified crops, returned the answers: environmental groups with 26 per cent, universities 6 per cent, national authorities 4 per cent and industry 1 per cent. The greater the public understanding through government and corporate expenditure on 'education', the firmer the rejection according to an editorial in *Nature* (5 August 1999, p. 499). What hope the new public relations body of the Australian Government, 'Biotechnology Australia'?

So how does the science we are all expected to understand, and which many debating current issues claim to have on their side, really work?

The popular biology writer Stephen Jay Gould follows the philosopher Karl Popper in defining science as a procedure for testing and rejecting hypotheses, not as a compendium of certain knowledge. Statements based on scientific evidence are made which are (or later turn out to be) false. However, as long as they can be tested in principle, they remain within the ambit of science. Thus, at any one time, science contains within its wide boundaries many claims that someone can and will prove wrong.

In stark contrast, theories that cannot be tested are, by this definition, not science. Science is doing, and not just clever thinking, clever debating or dogmatic believing.

So when *does* science eventually prove 'something'? When 'enough' men and women skilled in that art are collectively convinced by the evidence. But the jury is always out, and new evidence can be introduced at any time.

It depends on the field, but in practice, once material has survived several editions in the standard textbooks, about 90 per cent of it will remain unchallenged. It is hard for a dissenter to recall the jury. But every now and then, verdicts are changed. Even the experts cannot predict today, which ones might change tomorrow.

But society has to make decisions on the basis of current evidence. Courts have to reach forensic verdicts, medical boards have to introduce new treatments and drugs, farmers want access to new genetic technologies, decisions scream out to be made for investment in energy alternatives to fossil fuels. The level of scientific literacy in government fluctuates around zero and is not that much higher in the bureaucracy. Even the miserable level of funding for science awareness is under threat (except for high-profile but under-reported splurges like the Australia Prize).

Meanwhile, an under-informed public becoming over-anxious on issues is still assuaged by expensive 'education' and 'management' of remedial programs after a negative event. This costs thousands more than investment in good, upfront, honest exposure of how science really works in practice. But today's academic-industrial complex is mainly interested in 'industrially correct' research.

I was taught in school that Australia was a bountiful agricultural country 'ripe for exploitation'. Today we see the damage. We have introduced Landcare, Bushcare, Water Watch and so on. It's Time for (basic) science-care.

Churchill once said that he wanted his scientists 'on tap', not 'on top'. Fair enough. But here that tap is clogged up with economists and lawyers. Time for some caustic Draino.

Why *is* the whole more than the sum of the parts?

RELATING CAUSE and effect is something we do all the time. When things happen, we always look for an explanation. We need to know why. Either to sheet home blame or learn from the experience. Or, if the result was good, to repeat the circumstances. However, linking cause and effect is often surprisingly difficult. Let's see why with a sporting analogy.

Who is 'instrumental' in winning a football game? Is it the star player who scores the tries/goals? How important are the supporting roles? Isn't providing the 'break' often more crucial? And what about the referee, the crowd?

How predictable is the effect of player substitution? Not as good as selectors would like because the whole dynamics of the team may be changed. Teams are more than the sum of their players. Try rating team members from one to ten individually, and add up the total for each team. This score would be lucky to account for about half the actual results. Throw three dozen ambitious, fit men and a leather ball onto a field and the possibilities for surprise are enormous. Selectors and managers of teams in sport (or business for that matter) can't seem to predict much better than us non-professionals.

'Environment' is another factor. Recognising the effect of crowd response, European soccer offers twice as many competition points for a non-home ground win.

Scientists analyse the equivalent problems using terms such as 'degree of coupling', 'off-diagonal elements in the matrix', or 'non-linear effects'—not in a straight line, that is, not one-to-one. Theories of neural networks are the rage in computing.

The story is the same. Predictability is generally limited. Attempts to extract simple relations in some areas of the medical, economic and social sciences has been labelled 'physics envy', because classical physics is one of the few sciences to have predictable laws. (Even then, the three-piece pendulum—as seen in science centres—while obeying these laws, behaves chaotically because its motion is super-sensitive to tiny fluctuations in conditions.)

Now think about chemicals allegedly causing cancer. Sometimes the finger can be pointed at a particular chemical initiating a cancer but much cooperative activity from other chemicals (called promoters) is nearly always essential along the way.

Whether a cancer (or any disease) eventually 'scores' also depends very much on the efforts of the opposing 'team', the body's enzymes, repair and immune systems. The environment, including diet and lifestyle, has a strong role and can switch the game from home with a stadium full of fans for the immune system to away, yelled down in a foreign bear pit. The same argument applies to the drugs used to treat us.

And food too is more than the sum of its components. Hence, the intake of specific chemicals (vitamin pills, mineral supplements and the like) is seldom going to be as effective as a balanced diet of real food. Nutrition is also a major team effort.

A 'team' being more than the sum of its players is a universal phenomenon. Scientists call this effect the 'emergent properties' of a complex system; emerging, often unpredictable, from interactions between simple factors.

Simple, linear, one-to-one effects are not the rule in nature. They are overemphasised in the classroom because they are easier to teach. The media demands them because they are understandable, even if misleading.

Computer simulations can indeed give answers to 'what-if' type questions in complex systems. If the computer models are good, the predictions of consequences from particular assumptions are realistic. But modelling does not provide explanations. There is a big difference between prediction of consequences and an explanation.

We analyse complex non-linear situations by taking 'slices' through the data. We develop parameters within which we attempt to extract 'linear' relationships from the complexity.

Patterns from nowhere

Add 1 to 2 millimetres of cooking oil to a frying pan and heat gently. The surface becomes covered with polygon convection cells. To make the flow pattern which creates the cells really show up well, sprinkle a powdered spice, like cinnamon, onto the surface of the oil before heating. Thus a simple operation can give rise to a complex pattern.

The share market is a classic example, with its columns of market indicators. For failure, we create excuses, like player's off-day, fate, side effect, market sentiment/failure, collateral damage, etcetera.

A team is a typical complex system. The strong non-linear interactions between its members mean it is often impossible to assign improved (or declining) team performance to the input of individual team members. That's the fundamental management problem in work and play. It's also a major research area for scientists.

Sometimes we should be satisfied with the Eastern 'holistic' and 'community' approach to some of life's issues rather than always seeking rational 'one effect due to one cause' type of answers.

We keep trying to do so but shouldn't be surprised if we often get it wrong.

Epidemiology

The French Paradox

Worldwide there is a strong correlation between national wine consumption and recorded mortality from coronary heart disease. Consumption varies from a low 3 litres per person per year in Scotland and Finland to 100 litres per person per year in France—with a corresponding tenfold drop in mortality.

1 Set hypothesis.
  Moderate wine drinking is good for your health.

Pure versus applied

A young man and a young woman stand facing each other in opposite corners of a room. The man is allowed to move halfway across the room towards the woman. Then he can move half that distance again, and then half again, and so on.

A mathematician will say the man will never reach the woman (Zeno's paradox).

A statistician will say the man **will** reach the woman for all practical purposes.

2 Do a case control study.
Take a group of heart attack survivors and compare them to a carefully chosen similar (in every other way) group of people who have not had heart attacks. Compare the number of wine drinkers in each group. (Notoriously difficult to get honest drinking answers.)

3 Do a cohort study.
Take a homogenous group of people without any evidence of heart disease today and follow them for years (ten to fifteen). Compare the drinkers with the non-drinkers. (Needs researchers who will outlive the study group!)
A better study but no quick answers. You still have confounding factors such as that wine drinkers tend to have more smokers amongst them.

4 Do an interventionist trial.
Take a homogenous group and randomly make half drink alcohol and prevent the other half. This is the best method and is often used for testing drugs. However, not really a goer for wine drinking!

5 Finally, when you get a result like 180 out of 1000 die of the non-drinkers compared with 150 out of 1000 for drinkers, is this statistically significant? At what level do you accept the result?

When all the results are combined the answer seems to be that alcohol (from whatever source) is protective in the range 9 to 34 grams per day (10 grams of alcohol is one standard drink).

Black and white evidence

An engineer, an applied mathematician and a pure mathematician were travelling in a train in Switzerland. After a while the engineer said, 'I've seen many hundreds of cows out the window in the last hour and every one of them is black and white. In my opinion, all the cows in Europe must be black and white.'

The applied mathematician said, 'What nonsense, you can't conclude that. All you can say is that Swiss cows are all black and white.'

The pure mathematician was horrified. 'You are both extrapolating beyond the data. You can say no more than that the cows you have seen are all black and white.' And after looking out the window himself he added, 'And only on one side'.

Verdict first, trial afterwards

The professions all work within a particular paradigm which provides the rules for the correct way of doing things. These rules provide security for those operating within the group. In the 1970s a Turkish airlines DC-10 crashed. It was immediately assumed that this was an act of Kurdish terrorism. It was not credible that the design was so faulty that a cargo door just fell off, which was the conclusion finally reached. The same investigative progression occurred with the more recent crash of the TWA jet off the coast of the USA, where the FBI was primed to assume it was a bomb; instead it was shown to have probably been a fuel explosion allowed by a mechanical fault.

The classic modern scientific example was the non-discovery of the hole in the ozone layer where the automatic treatment of the data collected removed a number of points as outliers because they were too far off the expected curve on the graph. This illustrates a professional arrogance which seems to say 'we haven't seen this before, therefore it either doesn't exist or it must be a mistake.

HEALTH

Why 'Genes 'r' Us'

. . . Sharon had started asking The Question: 'Where did I come from Mummy?' As she patted her daughter's blonde hair (catalogue number: HC 205) and looked into her perfect cornflower blue eyes (catalogue number: EC 317), Tracy decided that, in the year 2095, there was nothing to be squeamish about . . .

Trevor and Tracy had gone to the Ideal Baby exhibition . . . combed through months of back issues of *Genes and Babies* magazine . . . window-shopped at the Swedish genetic superstore . . . What more could loving parents do for their child?

. . . [But] Sharon would always be less intelligent than Charlotte next door, whose grandparents had taken out a second mortgage to help purchase for her the genes guaranteeing ultra-intelligence (catalogue number: IQ 300) . . .'

'Genes 'R' Us', T. Wilke in G. Robertson et al. (eds),
FutureNatural: nature, science, culture, Routledge, London,
1996

HUMOUR IS OFTEN an excellent way of expressing our deepest fears. Biotechnology has caused many of us deep concerns. Its application to personal medical problems is likely to be accepted because there it is usually treating some terrible disease and in such cases it mostly affects only the individual. Its first applications to agriculture, however, have caused vigorous opposition—on social and ethical grounds—but chiefly because the initial benefits are to the farmer and producer and not directly to the general public. That was a major tactical error, as has since been admitted by the industry.

But let's have a look at the issues involved.

A crash course in molecular biology

For life forms other than viruses and prions, DNA is the basis of the genetic code. The holy mantra chants that the molecular double helix codes for genes with four different chemical 'letters'. This information is translated via RNA to make proteins. That is simplifying it a lot.

DNA is subject to quick changes by mutation separated by long periods of sameness. Sexual reproduction is the way most plants and animals fast forward the process and provide a mix of gene combinations in their offspring.

Simple life forms like bacteria can do something extra. They occasionally swap genes across species, like crossing cats and dogs. They don't do it often, but often enough to cause us severe problems.

As we overexposed bacteria to antibiotics, they mutated to resist our weapons and can now even destroy them. With their gene swapping they can also transfer these skills to unrelated bacteria. Our weapons against a wide range of diseases have thus quickly been rendered impotent.

We also overexposed bacteria to pesticides. These bacteria also mutated and some can now biodegrade the pesticides. However, genetic engineers have mimicked the natural process of cross-species transfer and cut and pasted the appropriate gene from these bacteria to crop plants to make the crop resistant to a broad spectrum herbicide and allow the herbicide to be sprayed safely while killing only the weeds. Thus, for example, the seeds for Monsanto's glyphosate-resistant crops will require more spraying with glyphosate (Zero or Roundup) but less of other much more questionable sprays. Farmers will, of course, be tied to Monsanto for seed and herbicide (glyphosate is out of patent but they may not be able to use generic products).

Our own DNA contains sequences from victories in the distant evolutionary past over disease; bits of DNA incorporated from the survivors of plagues of yesteryear. We don't really know why. We still need lots of answers.

Estimating the risk

There is so much we don't yet understand about genetics, and the simplistic approach of arguing (or regulating) the safety or otherwise of little bits of biotech science sequentially and in isolation—by taking slices of the data on these complex non-linear situations—may be a recipe for disaster.

So how can you estimate the safety of a new technology you don't understand? A look at your future home insurance policy might give you a clue. Since the mid-1970s an exclusion clause has been inserted relieving the insurer from liability resulting from civilian use of nuclear radiation (wars and insurrections are already excluded). If a similar clause arrives relating to gene technology, it also means that the risk is not estimable.

Whatever the final outcome, when the dust settles over the genetech wars, there will be collateral damage to science, industry and the regulatory system. Everyone working in these areas should (but won't) blame themselves for their refusal to consider other world views.

Consensus conference on gene technology in the food chain

Early in March 1999, a lay panel of citizens covering a wide range of ages, occupations and experience was selected at random through Australian newspaper advertisements. The panel members were briefed over two weekends on the technical background of gene technology. The panel then sat in the Senate chamber of the Old Parliament House in Canberra, across the benches from a group of experts the panel had selected. The role of experts was to respond to questions on which the panel had previously agreed, covering not only science, but also economics, trade and ethics.

As the experts at the Consensus Conference could only respond to the panel, not to each other, there was none of the vigorous debate that normally acts to separate out scientific fact from personal opinion and thus quickly corrects misleading or inaccurate presentation. It was argued that technical debate between duelling PhDs would be of no help to the lay person and was thus not included in the conference protocol. However, panellists did express a desire to see the experts sort out their differences in the same manner that was required of them in deliberations on the final report. The panel, which came out strongly in favour of comprehensive labelling of all gene modified food products, wished that the whole community could become as well informed as it now was. Interestingly, the panel's report was supported by the CEO of CSIRO, Dr Malcolm McIntosh, if not necessarily by some of his scientific staff. (The First Australian Consensus Conference: The People and Science meet Gene Technology, 10–12 March 1999. Copies of the report and follow-up are available from the Australian Consumers Association.)

The outcome of this first Australian Consensus Conference on Gene Technology in the Food Chain was to reinforce the findings of earlier research that showed the better informed people are about a controversial issue involving science and society, the more likely their disquiet will increase. Harvard academic W. W. Lowrance first noted this reaction in his classic *Of Acceptable Risk* (William Kaufmann, Los Altos, 1976).

Risk equals hazard plus outrage

In 1991, Peter Sandman of Rutgers University popularised this dichotomy between scientific calculation and public perceptions of risk in his formula for risk communication: Risk equals hazard plus outrage (sold as a video from the American Industrial Hygiene Association, Akron Ohio, 1991). He defined 'hazard' as what scientists call risk, and 'outrage' as a measure of how the public reacts to it. Surprisingly, Sandman suggests that social scientists can often predict the size of public outrage about an issue more accurately than physical scientists can realistically calculate its hazard in terms of mathematical odds. Sandman reworked Lowrance's criteria and ranked them. We apply some of these criteria to GMOs.

Voluntary versus involuntary

The genetech food debate scores extreme on the outrage scale. This outrage is the public's response to the discovery that it has involuntarily purchased products that may have involved genetic engineering. Voluntarily accepting a risk, compared with having it thrust upon one, can involve a thousandfold difference in outrage, according to Sandman.

Australia's food industry fought consumer advocates long and hard over 20 years, opposing the labelling of food products with ingredients. I know. I was the first consumer representative on the national Food Standards Committee. The arguments went as follows: ingredients in processed foods needed to be changed depending on market availability and price, and did ingredients matter anyway in products far removed from the starting ingredients, like wine and beer? (Pressure from brewers had beer exempted!)

They opposed drained weight: drained weight would depend on the size of the sieve. It would depend on the time of draining. Syrups made thick would drain too slowly.

They opposed food additives labelling: in spite of Australian exports at the time being available in European markets with mandatory additive codes, it seemed just too hard for the local cans.

They opposed alcohol content labelling: it would encourage consumers to buy the beer with the highest amount of alcohol.

They opposed country of origin labelling: what is the product? The raw materials, or the processing, or packaging?

These problems were solved.

On the other hand, industry had 'no worries' with nutritional labelling because this helps it to sell more products. Advertising panels may highlight folate content of breakfast cereals as a preventive measure against spina bifida in babies, even though its efficacy in this form has never been established by controlled epidemiology. And manufacturers are now pushing for further therapeutic-value labelling of food. Such hypocrisy further increases outrage.

Every day we see separation and labelling in the supermarkets of different varieties and origins of fruits and vegetables. Why not for genetech food? And when production of genetically enhanced corn for industrial proteins is in full swing, such as for avidin, widely used for bioanalytical applications, separation will be essential. (Avidin is a potent inhibitor of biotin, an essential vitamin, and accidental ingestion could be health threatening.) Costing $50 per kilogram compared with $1000 for conventional extraction from egg whites, this 'biopharming' will be highly lucrative. We'll soon have vaccines in bananas, vitamin A in rice and so on. Separation and labelling should be made the norm—now.

Substantially equivalent

Pure sugar made from a genetically engineered cane has no DNA left in it and therefore no trace of its origins. Where the production process is different but the products so made are not distinguishable by other than exotic analysis methods, industry wishes them to be defined as being 'substantially equivalent' and argues that they should not be separately labelled. Makes scientific sense.

However, acceptance of the concept of substantial equivalence will have other ramifications. Can imitation cosmetics be labelled as substantially equivalent to expensive French brands? Will athletes be able to justify the use of human hormones in sport with the same reasoning?

It is also clear that many shoppers want production information certified—the *process* is the *product*. They want to know whether the product is organic, halal, or for that matter whether their wine was made from grapes. By international agreement, irradiated food imported into Australia will be so labelled, even though it is only a process and often causes no substantial difference in the product.

Ethical framework

Consumers want choices based on their ethical framework and personal values and many resent developments—such as so-called 'terminator' genes. Indeed, the fight between the industrial–research complex and consumers has the hallmarks of an ethnic conflict, where each side has indoctrinated its followers with its interpretation of events to induce fear and loathing for the other side. It has been argued that traditional selective breeding has produced some terrible outcomes (in certain breeds of cats and dogs for example) while gene technology can produce quite

Terminator genes

Like hybrids, these modifications will render crop seed sterile by activating a 'killer' gene on ripening and thus maintain new seed sales for the next crop. While ensuring a return on the investment for the inventors, the practice will create special hardship in third world countries.

unique and focussed outcomes. Gene technology cannot be both just an extension of traditional breeding and at the same time provide fast and unlimited applications. Conflicting messages of this type inevitably breed conflict.

Cost benefit: whose cost and whose benefit?

A tomato has been modified to include a flounder gene? This enables the tomato to resist chilling and last six weeks in the industrial coolroom. However, the nutritional content goes down regardless, without any signs of the deterioration. This may be a gain to the seller but hardly to the buyer. (It at least answers the question: is a tomato a vegetable or a fruit? Neither, it's a fish!!)

Trust is a major factor in determining outrage

In Australia, the powerful food industry lobbied to have all the necessary assessments, from farm to plate, take place in agriculture departments. This overturns the status quo whereby health concerns are ruled on by the Health Department, environmental effects by the Environment Department, and so on. Currently, all of these departments are brought in to pass judgment on the relevant aspect of a problem, each of them trusted by a different sector of the community.

Australia, with its Commonwealth State bureaucracies, has a mixed record of successfully closing loopholes on regulation to ensure that what is Federal fiat is actually monitored and then enforced on the ground by the States and Territories.

It is about these very practical aspects of the new technology that I have the greatest concern, and four years spent as the head of a regulatory authority has taught me that having

Nice rice

If the first genetically modified (GM) product introduced had been saffron rice, the whole story might well have been different. Genetic modification can do things that conventional breeding cannot. Saffron rice has had seven new genes inserted over a period of seven years' research. This carrot-coloured rice has high levels of both iron and beta carotene (precursor for vitamin A). Vitamin A deficiency affects 400 million people worldwide making them susceptible to infections and blindness. Iron anaemia occurs in some three billion people, mainly women.

The research was carried out in the public domain and so the results are available free. No royalties, no terminator genes, and what is more, labelled by colour (non-removable by washing!). Ergo, no grounds for protest.

committed, competent and dedicated scientists is not enough to head off problems. If, as the industry argues, it is too difficult to maintain the so-called 'identity preservation' needed to label genetically modified products, and given the financial attractiveness of biopharming, I really worry. Eating an avidin-producing bioplant will cause immediate biotin (an essential vitamin) deficiency. Extraction of a small quantity of valuable chemical will leave large quantities of waste plant material behind. Hopefully this will not be sold as cheap feed to the beef industry to jeopardise exports yet again! Can it be composted safely? And what else will little bioplants produce for us in the future? What other problems?

At the very least

We might have expected those with most to gain from a new technology to come forward and say how worried they are about any possible collateral damage, no matter how remote. We might have expected them to say: 'We have invested tens of millions in this technology. The country stands to earn squillions. We do worry about all those issues you have brought up. We freely admit we don't understand all the wider social ramifications of our work, and we'll willingly discuss matters that concern us all. Give us some good ideas on how they should be tackled. We shall listen carefully to what you are telling us and spend day and night trying to devise and support mechanisms which decrease your outrage and build your trust.'

Sadly, once mistrust sets in, the world tends to be viewed through conspiracy-tinted glasses. But it is unlikely that industry will blame itself for failure—it is much easier to blame the activists and media and think the answer is better education or management of the public.

Why Mandrake makes magic

OK, SO WE don't like our food stuffed around by these gene engineers. You don't know what they might do to you. So let us all stick to *natural*, *organic* produce. If it was good enough for our ancestors to survive on, it is good enough for us.

Then on the still night air,
The bark of a dog is heard,
A shriek! A groan!
A human cry. A trumpet sound.
The Mandrake root lies captured on the ground.

According to this 'eye-witness account' of the uprooting of a mandrake root from the Middle Ages, the dog had wax in its ears to avoid the plant's alleged madness-inducing shriek as it was uprooted.

Mandrake has a long association with murder, magic and medicine (a book by that name, by John Mann [Oxford University Press, 1992] inspires this section). Mandrake root contains tropane alkaloids, principally atropine and hyoscine. Alkaloids are organic compounds containing nitrogen which are produced by plants as natural insecticides. The nitrogen is positively charged in water, and this is the basis of their effect on humans and other animals. Depending on the dose, alkaloids can have toxic, euphoric or anaesthetic effects.

'On certain days or nights [witches] anoint themselves under the arms and other hairy places, and ride on a staff to the appointed place,' Mann writes. 'The ointments and salves so used by witches were prepared using extracts from mandrake, deadly nightshade or henbane, all of which contain hyoscine, mixed with animal fat. The sweat glands and fine blood capillaries at "hairy places" allow alkaloids to penetrate slowly into the bloodstream. In this way high levels reached the brain, without passage of large amounts through the gut with attendant risk of poisoning'. (See p. 146 on sunscreens.)

Today, hyoscine is used (in mixtures) as a pre-medication before operations and in tablets (now called scopolamine) to prevent motion sickness. It can also be taken through the skin with skin patches, mimicking the witches' method.

A related alkaloid, Atropine comes from deadly nightshade, and its ability to enlarge the pupils in the eye allegedly made ladies more attractive and hence led to its name 'belladonna'. Ophthalmologists used it until better synthetics were recently developed. Along with mandrake, deadly nightshade belongs to the solanaceae family, as do potato, tomato and tobacco.

Sunlight produces toxic levels of alkaloids in potatoes, luckily with a coincident warning through photosynthetic greening, unless the food is irradiated to prevent sprouting, in which case the warning but not the poison disappears!.

Atropine is used as a temporary antidote to poisoning from organophosphates (OP) and until recently was mentioned in the first aid instructions on OP household pesticides. (See Rogor on p. 43.) It is still given in emergency packs to the military if exposure to nerve poisons is expected. Nerve poisons work by stopping the reset of nerves, keeping them firing and limbs and muscles moving chaotically until you die. The resetting job is normally done by an enzyme that breaks down the chemical 'transmitter' acetylcholine once a message has been relayed. Atropine blocks nerve cell receptors and stops excess acteylcholine from triggering them, thus acting as an antidote to nerve poisons.

As the witches had long known, in excess all these natural compounds cause unnatural activation of nerve endings, which can lead to altered states of awareness.

Now move to the present and we find ourselves in a pleasant, natural springtime country scene in New Zealand—evoked by the following riddle:

Q: What has six legs and goes around in a circle?
A: A ram doing a ewe.

Suddenly there is a clap of thunder and the ewes start mounting the rams instead. The Kiwi farmers panic!

In the early 1970s, this was first observed on certain improved pastures in Australia and called sheep clover disease. The fear that the ewes had been reading Germaine Greer and become liberated feminists was not the issue, rather the lack of issue; the ewes had become sterile.

It turned out the cause was a natural phytoestrogen from introduced pasture clovers, which acts as a powerful contraceptive in ewes, destroying cervical cells and thus preventing sperm from entering. Extracted, purified, and in the right amount, it is useful for female humans and as Promensil became one of the best sellers for a local pharmaceutical company Novogen, which sold the extract of red clover (*Trifolium pratense*) as a natural hormone replacement. The product contains isoflavones, and the label states the amount of active extract present in each tablet.

Another plant, echinacea, is a native of America, and *Chemistry in Australia* reports that its extracts are the most popular medicinal herb sold in Australia. Echinacea is supposed to promote the body's immune system. Once a traditional naturopath item, it has now found respectability in pharmacies as well as supermarkets.

Analysis of 32 brands of echinacea products showed reasonable consistency between samples of the same brand but the variation between different brands was enormous. Echinacea products are labelled only with the amount of plant material extracted. Not on the label is the amount of active components present. The greatest variation in active components ranged from 0 to 3.8 milligrams per gram for alkylamides and 0 to 14.7 milligrams per gram for caffeoyl phenols.

Why so much variation? Not because different producers used different amounts of plant material for their extract. Nor that the sources of plants caused the variation. No. It was the skill applied to the extraction of active ingredients. Some components are harder to extract and more vulnerable to degradation during preparation than others. The skill of the chemist determines the quality of the product.

So just reading the label for how much herb it contains will tell you very little about how much active component you'll swallow. And unlike the hormone replacement product, you can't even test the activity of echinacea on your pet lamb beforehand. Tough!

What is the moral in all this?

Once you undertake an extraction of a natural material, you deliberately select certain ingredients and reject others and change their relative amounts. Their very nature may be subtly changed by the extraction and concentration processes. And you upset the balance of all the myriad chemicals that are in the original. This is what extraction does. Can this sort of product, then, really claim to be 'natural'? I think not.

Why say NO for sex?

LAST CENTURY DOCTORS recommended rubbing nitroglycerine (a component of gelignite) on the chest or inhaling amyl nitrite to mitigate an attack of angina (a painful spasm from overexerting a weak heart). Nobody knew why it worked, not even Sherlock Holmes (see *The Case of the Resident Patient*). The first clue came in World War I with the surprising observation that ammunition packers had very low blood pressure. Nitric oxide (NO—an atom of oxygen linked to one of nitrogen) was soon found to be the agent, relaxing the constricting muscles around the heart. A form of NO occurs in both nitroglycerine and amyl nitrite.

Sodium nitrite—which is formed from salt and dung and is a source of NO—has been used since prehistoric times to preserve meat—again without any understanding of how it worked.

Students make NO in the chemistry lab by treating copper filings with concentrated nitric acid (with air absent). Nitric oxide (NO) and ozone are formed when electricity discharges in air—that's what you smell around crackling power lines. Atmospheric lightning provides a large proportion of the nitrates essential to plant life by first forming NO, which then reacts further. Around badly serviced photocopying machines, the same two gases—NO and ozone—can cause breathing problems.

Twenty years ago it was realised NO was a significant component of car exhaust. NO is reactive with oxygen and forms other (brown) oxides, a major component in photochemical smog.

Ten years ago, it was realised that our bodies produce small but essential quantities in macrophages (cells found in the blood). These inject NO into invading microbes and mutant cells to kill them. But too much NO production in a good cause can induce septic shock from excess lowering of blood pressure, so we routinely breathe out NO at a concentration of 8 parts per billion.

The climax of the role of NO came in 1991 when it was found to be released in the spongy muscle of the penis during sexual arousal, relaxing that muscle to allow blood to enter and swell the tissues. NO appears to be the prime mover (so to speak) for erections.

A Viagra tablet is much more convenient than packing some gelignite around the local member. But take care, there is extra reinforcement when a person on nitro treatment for angina takes Viagra as well. The combination can kill.

So NO news is good (and bad) news. It's the right dose and in the right place that counts. NO wonder.

Antibiotic resistance: whose fault?

A COMMONWEALTH GOVERNMENT committee reported yet again (September 1999) on the increasing resistance to antibiotics of the microbes that threaten our health. Sooner rather than later our abuse of antibiotics will go critical and we'll wonder how we could have been so stupid.

Virtually every professional journal has had reports over the last five years on the increasing spread of antibiotic resistance amongst the disease bugs. Newspapers and television have provided dramatic warnings. Stuart B. Levy wrote a clear and thoughtful book in 1992, *The Antibiotic Paradox: how miracle drugs are destroying the miracle* (Plenum Press NY) and followed it up with an article in *Scientific American* two years ago.

Veterinarians and doctors have been at each others' throats over this issue for decades and this is the root cause of inaction. Medicos blame the vets for using valuable antibiotics not only for treating animal sickness but also to boost production in the intensive animal farming industries. Two-thirds of the antibiotics imported into Australia are used on animals, the other one-third on humans. We imported 14 tonnes of avoparcin for animals in 1995–96 for use in stockfeed, principally for pigs and poultry. The practice of using antibiotics in stockfeed arose when spent by-products of fermentations that were used to produce the antibiotic aureomycin (chlortetracycline) in 1949 were used as a cheap source of Vitamin B12 for stock. The vitamin turned out to be unimportant but the trace of antibiotic left in the mash did wonders.

However, low-level use of antibiotics may contribute to

bacterial resistance to that antibiotic then higher amounts must be used for the same production boost in the animal. In the case of avoparcin, bacteria resistant to it may also be resistant to vancomycin, the human antibiotic of last resort, because it is chemically similar to avoparcin and works the same way. Or they may transfer this resistance to other disease-causing microbes. This makes the community more vulnerable to infection for which there is limited treatment.

There is little the individual can do. Avoiding meat doesn't help because it is not a direct transfer from animal to human (by contact or food) that is important (except in the immuno-compromised), but a change in the overall population of microbes to which we are all exposed. A study of Seventh Day Adventists in California (NHMRC 1996 report) who eschew meat showed they have similar levels of resistant gut microbes as a control group they were tested against.

There is wide disparity in regulations controlling antibiotic use in animal feed. In Australia we don't allow the fluorquinolines or the amphenicols, colisitin or gentamicin (aminoglycosides), and cephalosporins have only been allowed sine the mid-1990s; most other countries have been using these for the last fifteen to twenty years. Since a review in the late 1980s, Carbodox has been prohibited because of its cancer-causing potential, but it is still allowed in Europe, Canada and the United States. We do allow virginiamycin, but related antibiotics are now used for human multi-resistant infections and it has been restricted in Europe. Penicillin is banned from stockfeed here (but not for treating animal infection), but not in the United States. Although not an antibiotic, and not used in humans, arsenic compounds are used here and in the United States to boost animal production.

Interestingly, avoparcin has never been licensed or used in animal husbandry in the United States, yet the United States has one of the widest prevalence of bacterial resistance to vancomycin. This has given the vets one of their best arguments.

So the vets have been blaming the medicos for 50 years of indiscriminate, inappropriate and over-prescribing of antibiotics. Australians use more antibiotics per head than every developed country except France, although there seems to be a slight levelling off here, but not overseas. By prescribing for virus infections (for which antibiotics don't work) and not ensuring that a course of treatment is taken right through, no matter how good the patient feels (which allows the surviving bugs to build up resistance), doctors also connive in the overall bacterial triumph. Not waiting to test for the type of infective agent before prescribing and using a broad spectrum antibiotic eventually loses us a valuable weapon. Doctors do have a duty of care to an individual patient, but they also have one to the community as a whole. Being more than on the safe side for the individual (or just lazy) can increase the risk for the wider community, again by selectively breeding resistant microbes for all of us.

Hospitals have been the major source of resistant bacteria. Anyone who has been seriously infected after surgery and watched the staff pump one antibiotic after another into their veins knows the feeling of vulnerability that this loss of antibiotic potency induces.

The last time the National Health and Medical Research Council (NHMRC) reported on this issue (November 1996), the scientific evidence weighed heavily against medical overuse and questioned veterinary use in animal feed, although the moral high ground (i.e. more emotive argument on television) was held by the medicos. I was chair of the National Registration Authority for Agricultural and Veterinary Chemicals (NRA) at the time. Unlike most overseas organisations, the NRA and its predecessors have conducted evaluations of antibiotic resistance in animal use for 30 years.

We, the public, are now well informed about overuse of antibiotics and if we don't take an active part in the debate we may, in the end, need to blame ourselves when our resources have run out. Demanding an antibiotic script when inappropriate *is* inappropriate. We can search for produce that is certified free from the use of feed antibiotics (or hormones, or genetically modified organisms, or whatever else we feel strongly about), provided that appropriate labelling is available. While using antibiotics for the seemly crass purpose of boosting primary production slightly seems irresponsible, it would appear that stopping this practice will have little impact on the problem.

Avoparcin has been withdrawn from use in Europe. With the market having shrunk it is no longer economic to sell it in Australia and so the manufacturer will cease to register and market here. Nice to have a problem solved for one.

Further Information

On antibiotic resistance in general (Stuart Levy), see http://www.sciam.com/
1998/0398issue/0398levy.html. On vancomycin operation and resistance, see
http://tuna.dp.ox.ac.uk/~martin/chemtech/resistance.html.

Report of the Joint Expert Committee on Antibiotic Resistance (JETACAR),
*The Use of Antibiotics in Food-Producing Animals: Antibiotic resistant bacteria in
animals and humans*, Commonwealth Departments of Health and Agriculture, Canberra, September 1999.

Adrien asks: is it food, drug or poison?

XENOBIOSIS: FOOD, DRUGS *and Poisons In the Human Body* is a title of a book by Adrien Albert, one-time professor of medical chemistry at the Australian National University. It describes chemicals that can act as food, drugs or poisons in the human body, depending on circumstances. *Xenobiotic* is coined from the Greek *xenos* and *bios* (stranger to life). That is, those things which are foreign to the metabolic network operating in the human body.

The first question is: what is 'foreign'? The second question is: what is 'in'? The answer to the first question is: all components of the chemical environment; everything that is not us. And the answer to the second is that a substance inserted into an orifice of the human body cannot be *in* the body until it crosses a semi-permeable membrane.

The next question then is: how much of something does what?

> Wenn ihr Gift recht auslegen wolt, was ist, das nit Gift ist? Alle Dinge sind Gift, und nichts ist ohne Gift; allein die Dosis machts, dass ein Ding kein Gift sei. Zu exemplar, ein jegliche Speise und ein jeglich Getränk, wenn es über seine Dosis eingenommen wird, so ist es Gift; das beweist sein Ausgang. Ich gebe auch zu, dass Gift Gift sei; dass es aber darum verworfen werden solle, das darf nicht sein.
>
> Paracelsus (1493–1541)

What Paracelsus said in so many (German) words is: 'It is all a matter of dose.' The same substance can be a food, a medicine or a poison.

- *Oxygen* We need the 20 per cent in air to breathe. At higher concentration oxygen finds cautious use in medicine, but pure oxygen is dangerous. (We absorb about 250 millilitres per minute from the air, bind 19 millilitres per 100 millilitres in the haemoglobin in the blood, and carry only a tiny amount, 0.3 millilitres per 100 millilitres, as *free* oxygen.) Oxygen can thus be a food, a medicine or a poison.

What is the difference between a food and a drug? Caffeine and bran both have no food value and are eaten with different motives. When vitamins, minerals, antioxidants or whatever are extracted from the food in which they occur they are then drugs.

- *Plant poisons* Plants cannot flee their predators which has put them under continuous evolutionary pressure to secure their survival by chemical means. They accumulate many kinds of substances to repel or discourage micro-organisms, insects and grazing animals, including man. About 40 000 years ago, cooking was discovered as a great detoxifying process. In particular, it detoxified proteins (lectins and protease inhibitors) almost universally present in legumes (beans, peas and lentils), and in grains. Cooking also volatilises irritating volatile oils and destroys chemicals that produce hydrogen cyanide (cyanogenic toxins).

- *Alcohol* is metabolised slowly in the liver at a fixed rate (60–200 milligrams per kilogram body mass per hour) to acetaldehyde. So if you weigh 70 kilograms, you can take alcohol through the first stage of detoxifying at 4 to 14 grams per hour—that is, give or take, a standard drink of 10 grams.

  There is then further oxidation to carbon dioxide. Alcohol is readily converted to fat but cannot be converted to glucose or glycogen. For that reason it cannot be oxidised on demand like glucose and so is useless for emergency energy needs. Like pure sugar, it does not come along with the supply of vitamins (co-enzymes) that are needed by the body to deal with it. Hence there is a strong nutritional argument that we should fortify alcoholic drinks with thiamine. This would prevent thiamine deficiency when excess alcohol is consumed. We already do so with bread.

  The body can only store a small quantity of glycogen (about 160 grams) which is converted to glucose for our energy needs. The brain uses glucose (about 120 grams per day) as its exclusive fuel. Alcohol cannot supply any of this.

- *Lipids (fats)*   Most of the lipids released during a meal are dispatched into the bloodstream and soon disappear into the adipose tissue, which is a substantial protein network that extends from the ankle to the cheeks, and contains fat. When this adipose tissue is fully loaded it weighs 8 to 20 kilograms in normal healthy adults. In response to signals from the liver, enzymes called lipases in the adipose tissue liberate fatty acids from the fats. These fatty acids, coated with a protein (albumin), travel in the bloodstream to the requesting organs.

  The principal fatty acids of human adipose tissue are oleic (48%) and palmitic (23%). The fats you eat are broken down and resynthesised the way the body wants them. The poly-unsaturated linoleic acid (7%) must be obtained from the diet.

  Health is defined by the World Health Organisation as 'a state of complete physical, mental and social wellbeing and not merely the absence of disease'. Excess (fat) is defined as that which is associated with an increased death rate.

- *Sugar*   Sucrose can be poisonous in high doses. For example, in a study reported by Albert when female rats were fed increasing amounts of sugar, half the group died when the diet of sugar reached a level of 28 grams per kilograms of body mass which, in human terms, means a 10 kilogram child eating 225 grams of lollies at one sitting.

- *Proteins*   Plants can synthesise all of the twenty amino acids that combine to form most of the proteins, but humans can make only ten. The other ten (essential) amino acids must be consumed around the time that the body synthesises its protein needs. Too little and too much are both undesirable.

- *Salt*   is not found much in 'natural' food (mostly in meat). We ingest most of our salt as an additive in manufactured food or when we add it ourselves. About 20 per cent of the population gets (genetically determined) high blood pressure from excess salt. Potassium chloride can be substituted, but at high doses (about 18 grams) it is toxic.

- *Iron*   Iron is closely controlled by the body. It is recycled within an almost closed system and is very poisonous in excess. Normal men lose about 28 milligrams of iron per month (10 per cent of the total taken in every year), while women lose an extra 28 milligrams per month through menstrual blood.

- *Phytic acid*   This is found in bran and oatmeal, and it forms strong links and immobilises calcium, iron and zinc, which prevents the body using these crucial minerals. The enzyme phytase occurs in bread yeast and is also induced in the body to inactivate phytic acid to some extent, and release these minerals.

- *Potatoes*   On chemical analysis potatoes reveal at least 150 different substances, some of which are decidedly undesirable. Cooking induces more products. While introduced to Europe as late as 1570, potatoes had undergone around 4000 years of testing in Peru. This long period of biological testing has been (mostly) favourable. The normal level of the toxic alkaloid solanine is 30 to 60 milligrams per kilogram of potatoes, which adds up to a yearly intake of about 8 grams. Greening and sprouting are indicators of high local levels of solanine. (These sections should be cut out of potatoes.) Cooking does not destroy the compound. However, it is rapidly excreted. When poor growing or storing conditions increase the normal amount by a factor of ten, diarrhoea sets in along with difficulties in breathing, and continued high intake results in a coma. For pregnant women, excess solanines create a risk to the unborn child.

- *Pineapples*   These are rich in methanol and essences which easily revert to methanol. As little as 4 milligrams of methanol has caused permanent blindness; the accepted maximum recommended legal level in food is 2 milligrams per kilogram. Pineapples almost certainly exceed this. Don't eat too many at a time.

- *Nitrate*   In soils nitrate increases productivity and nitrate fertilisers are commonly used. Organic fertilisers convert to nitrate before being absorbed. However, in dry weather, sodium nitrate accumulates in crops, particularly spinach, but also beets, cabbage, carrots, celery, lettuce and radishes. Adults are not at immediate risk (although there is fear about the formation of carcinogenic nitrosamines).

Potassium nitrate was once prescribed as a diuretic (1 gram per day) and the side effects were mainly physical weakness and mental inertia. In 1935, spinach replaced the very toxic mercury compounds as a quieting agent for babies with teething and other problems. But infants under four months have low stomach acid, which allows bacteria to grow and which reduces nitrate to nitrite. This can lock up the haemoglobin and exclude uptake of oxygen with serious consequences (methaemoglobinaenemia). In the 1960s high nitrate intake was (slowly) discouraged.

- *Vitamin C*   In large doses, Vitamin C has claimed benefits ranging from combating colds to inhibiting cancer, but excessive amounts can lead to dependence, and if the intake is suddenly reduced to 'normal', scurvy can occur. This can happen in babies weaned from mothers taking too much.

- *Lectins*   These occur in the bean family and react with the cells lining the intestinal tract, reducing the absorption of nutrients and unchecked eventually leading to starvation. Those in peas and lentils appear to be harmless, those in soya beans less so, and in kidney beans lectins are highly toxic and need to be removed. *P. vulgaris* has many cultivars: kidney, white, black, navy, wax, haricot, and these provide the 'baked [Boston] bean'.

  The lectin from castor-oil seeds is deadly at 10^{-11} grams per kilogram of body mass—one of the most poisonous natural substances. (The Bulgarian secret police used this poison on the end of an umbrella to murder one of their own diplomats, playwright George Markov, in London in 1978.)

- *Pure distilled water*   Given to albino rats at the rate of 70 millilitres per kilogram every 20 minutes, pure distilled water had an LD_{50} of 470 millilitres per kilogram (body mass). LD_{50} is the dose at which half of the sample of rats tested died. To extrapolate this to humans means multiplying the dose (470 millilitres) by the ratio of the body mass of humans to rats (around 200) to give about 100 litres of water. Most of these animals died in a coma in two and a half hours. Excreting the extra water caused loss of salt, finally preventing conduction of impulses by the nerves. In humans water intoxication can occur after major surgery or in the presence of certain diseases.

For king, country
and chemical!

WHEN THE GERMAN company Bayer ceased exports to Australia at the beginning of World War I, the Australian Government suspended the company's local trademarks.

On 17 September, 1915, Billy Hughes, then Federal Attorney-General, announced 'that a sample of aspirin [acetyl salicylic acid, ASA] made in Australia was purer than the German product' and was to be manufactured by Messrs Shmith and Nicholas under the award of a new patent and use of the trade name Aspirin. 'The public should refrain from purchasing the German drug both from patriotic and prudent motives,' Hughes continued. But within two years, lobbying by British importers had led the Government to renege and cancel the trademark. Chemists haven't trusted governments ever since!

Although aspirin is not explosive, during his two years' work, Nicholas managed to blow up his pharmacy, and although not toxic at ordinary doses, he nearly managed to poison himself.

Pharmacist George Nicholas and industrial chemist Harry Shmith formulated their product as a tablet, first from a suspension in ether and later, more safely, with a dry granulation process. If exposed to moisture, pure aspirin soon reeks of acetic acid (vinegar) and grows fine crystals of salicylic acid on the surface. Anyone downing such a dose of old aspirin for a hangover is likely to suffer more than usual stomach irritation.

Copying the operation of a US seed planting device which stuck seeds onto a tape then waxed and planted them, tablets were first marketed in 1921 in individually wrapped wax pouches, trademarked Aspro. This was the forerunner of the modern foil strip. Joined by a manic, eccentric New Zealand advertising genius, George T. Davis, Aspro became a household name around the globe.

In World War II, Australian troops in South Asia quickly became victims of the tropical diseases malaria, dysentery, scrub typhus as well as streptococcal, gonococcal and pneumococcal infections. The uncertainty of continued supply of the new effective sulfa drugs prompted the Australian Government to encourage local production.

In 1942 Monsanto Chemicals produced commercial quantities of sulfanilamide from ammonia (supplied by ICIANZ in Victoria), aniline (from Timbrol in NSW), alcohol (from CSR in Queensland) and chlorosulfonic acid (from Government Fertilizers in Victoria).

Sulfaguadine was desperately needed to combat dysentery in New Guinea, but none was available in Australia. It was synthesised initially from sulfanilamide by two Sydney University chemists. The first batches played a vital role in the battle of the Kokoda Trail and later production went to British forces in Burma and India.

Supplies of quinine from the bark of a tropical tree of the Cinchona family used for treating malaria, were cut off by the advance of Japanese forces. Sulfamerazine was an effective synthetic alternative. An eight-step synthesis, which required exquisite glass-lined equipment, was developed at the University of Adelaide and commercialised by ICIANZ. Horrendous problems, ranging from fire to fouling of filters, were overcome.

An improvement in drug trialling protocol was introduced, whereby instead of the usual unwary randomly chosen mental patients, 900 healthy young soldiers unexposed to malaria were treated and then exposed to infection.

Adrien Albert, at the ANU, produced the first synthetic drug by an Australian to be included in the British Pharmacopoeia. It was 9-aminoacridine, developed during the war as a more powerful bacteriostat than the then popular yellow-staining acriflavine. It was the first drug found to attach itself to DNA and thereby stop bacteria from reproducing.

Though the Nicholas group survives, aspirin is no longer made in Australia. Sadly, Australia today imports most of its chemical needs to the detriment of our balance of payments and making us vulnerable to globalised decisions. We are going to need our own innovative chemists again one day.

Germany lost its patent on aspirin because of the war and Australia lost its patent through British pressure. It is surpising how many European patents the United States has 'appropriated'. Yet today US companies are outraged when third world countries suggest something similar for materials strategic to their needs, such as anti-AIDS drugs.

Further Information

For (much) more on Aspirin see Charles C. Mann & Mark L. Plummer, *The Aspirin Wars: money, medicine, and 100 years of rampant competition*, Alfred A. Knopf, New York, 1991, p. 420ff.

How well do you know your cupboard's chemicals?

THIS WEEKEND I spent an hour making soap. That's lovely you say, nice, green domestication. Well not really. I sprayed the inside of an oven coated with layers of fat with an aerosol containing over 4 per cent caustic soda. The caustic splits and reacts with the fat, releasing glycerine and forming mainly sodium stearate (common soap). Both products are water-soluble and easily washed away. Caustic soda is nasty stuff. It will turn the skin into soap too. And do irreparable damage to the eyes. The only other domestic product that comes near it in danger is machine dishwashing powder (which is not a detergent), the most common cause of child domestic trauma.

In 1990 the Commonwealth Department of Health commissioned a national survey of chemicals used in the home and the community's understanding of their hazards (by Reark Research). It started with thirteen focus groups, followed by a national door-to-door survey of 2677 people aged fourteen years and over (2500 adults, 100 aged 14–17, and 77 people of non-English speaking background). In addition, home audits of the storage of domestic chemicals were undertaken in 513 homes (20%). The survey found:

- One in every four adults was unable to spontaneously recall any household chemical which might harm an adult if accidentally used.
- More than four in five (86%) households frequented by under four-year-olds were found on audit to be storing hazardous household chemicals in an unsafe manner (unsafe

= accessible and stored unlocked below 1.5 metres). This was true in households where the head reported that they always read the label and took warnings seriously.

- Ninety-seven per cent of all households audited were found to be storing at least one chemical product unsafely.
- From a list of twenty, the seven items most commonly classified by users as 'fairly harmless' included four which would kill a child with a small dose.
- Evaluation by the public of likely outcomes of a series of chemical intakes showed no significant correlation with medical evaluations.
- Many chemical-product users were more likely than not to underestimate the seriousness of outcomes.
- People generally don't read labels either prior to using the product or even after an accident.

An Australian Institute of Health 1990 report, 'Accidental Poisoning by Household Chemicals', estimated that around 7000 people present at emergency departments at hospitals each year as a result of accidental poisoning by these products, with pharmaceutical drugs accounting for 60 per cent of cases. Australian Bureau of Statistics surveys show that 191 deaths resulted in 1998.

Some of the products the experts in poisoning considered moderately safe but the public thought were dangerous included: antibiotics, fabric softener, Valium tablets, asthma tablets, oral contraceptives, and white oil. Some of the products the experts considered dangerous but the public thought were not so bad included: camphor blocks, eucalyptus oil, anti-flea dog-wash, white wine, and iron tablets.

Dangerous products, like automatic dishwasher powder, superglue, mothballs, and less problematic products, like weed-killer and washing up detergent, were often gauged correctly. How good are you?

Do real rotters have a sense of humus?

ALL WAS QUIET on the home front. The November rains had brought out fresh red growth on the roses and eucalypts. But we knew the war was about to start again. The scarab beetle legions had dug in under the grass and were about to emerge as squadrons of leaf-eating Christmas beetles.

We moved into our treeless new residence twenty years ago. Our children insisted we plant a tree so that Delilah, the cat, would have somewhere to scramble up if chased by a dog. We tried to explain that trees are a very long-term investment in cat safety. We were wrong. Big Nic, as the nicholae eucalypt was soon to be called (although it turned out to be a peppermint gum—you can never trust the label), had found himself a stormwater channel and quickly grew to 30 metres or so, dwarfing all around. The cat never did take to flight into his generous limbs, but the local possums vocalised throatily there on many nights. The fallen leaves collect in the house gutters.

'Do something, you're a chemist', came the order each year as we all anticipated the destruction by the Christmas beetles. There is no point being a pacifist in the face a relentless enemy. To hell with the Geneva Convention. Chemical warfare is the answer.

I had become a household hero some time before when I injected neat Rogor (methoate) with a syringe into an indoor plant which had become infected with a hard white scale that was quickly killing it. Within a week it flexed its arboreal muscles, threw off the scale and thought it was a triffid. Note: using pesticides contrary to the instructions is *ILLEGAL*. But if you never read the instructions, you'll never never know. If you are going to break the rules take much more care with the safety aspects!

But back to the Nic. Spraying was out of the question. Armed with a hand drill and a 3 millimetre bit, I drilled some holes at a downward angle into the trunk of Big Nic at intervals of about ten centimetres around the circumference, through the bark and into the sap tissue. Rogor is not recommended for fruit trees, or any trees with foliage eaten by koalas or stock. However it doesn't harm birds eating the insects.

The sap carries the insecticide up into the branches and leaves where it is ingested by sucking and eating predators. The insecticide ends up where you want it, in the leaves, rather than all over the neighbour's garden, or blown back in your face. Hazard is about how you use a material as well as the nature of the material itself. The insecticide Rogor is designed to chemically self-destruct in a few weeks into harmless components so no permanent effect is left behind.

The organophosphorus insecticides, of which Rogor is an example, are nerve poisons. We saw on page 23 how nerve poisons work by binding almost permanently to the site where the acetylcholinesterase enzyme works, thus preventing it from removing the chemical 'transmitter' acetylcholine once it has done its job. Acetylcholine accumulates at the nerve junctions making transmissions impossible. The result is uncontrolled nerve firing to the muscles which control breathing and heart beat, followed by rapid death.

Unlike insects, mammals have enzymes which can detoxify these poisons. Provided your liver is functioning adequately and you don't suffer from asthma, organophosphorus insecticides do not present much risk. However, it takes only a minor change in the design of the compound to also prevent our enzymes from being able to detoxify it. Then we end up like the insect. The change is so small that were I to draw up the formulas for pesticides and nerve gases, it would take you some time to note the differences. This minor difference distinguishing an insecticide from a nerve gas was discovered the hard way by the chemist who first worked with these compounds in Germany in 1937. He 'lost' several of his research staff while learning about these chemicals.

Because of the similarities in the chemistry of organophosphate pesticides and nerve gases, the chemical plant used to make both of these products is the same. The only difference is in the protection methods built into the later stages of the nerve gas plant, which are far in excess of those needed for pesticide manufacture. Because of the extreme toxicity of nerve gases, the very last step of manufacture is often left undone and the final mixing occurs in the shell or bomb itself after release. These are called binary weapons. Many products use the same principle of final mix of components just before use, but not for safety reasons. Chemical light sticks mix the components just before you want them to glow. The two pack Araldite adhesive and polyurethane varnish are other examples.

In the case of the manufacture of nerve gas, the separate binary components represent little hazard, and their production need not be geographically close, and could in many cases each be linked to legitimate uses. This makes it difficult for international monitoring.

I share the abhorrence of war gases—such as chlorine and phosgene which act only through the lungs and cause fluid to collect in the lung and drown the victim. Mustard gas, too, which causes a slow, painful, disfiguring death to its victims is gruesome—although the mustards are now used carefully in anti-cancer therapy.

However, of all the rules we make for our social existence, the rules(?) of warfare must be the most bizarre. One of the (few) things I remember from National Service training (in the 1950s, when such things were compulsory), was the technique we were taught for bayoneting—twist the bayonet in the wound to let air in! However, woe betide anyone who had a rusty bayonet, because that could cause blood poisoning and render the bayonetter a war criminal.

The different nerve gases, sarin, tabun and soman, stockpiled during the last World War are toxic at levels of about one-tenth of a milligram. They were not used then but have been used since. Sarin was the nerve gas used in the Japanese subway attack on 20 March 1995, and by Iraq against Iran in 1984 and against its own Kurdish population in 1986.

Protection against nerve gases is straightforward in principle. A complete barrier between the gas and the body is needed (not just the lungs), along with a chemical filter for breathing air. The British have developed a 'Noddy' suit, which is expected to give protection for up to 24 hours of continuous use. It has a head mask sealed at the neck to prevent loosening as a beard grows. It has a massive array of filters, including asbestos and glass fibres, to filter out aerosols, followed by activated charcoal and mixtures of chromium, copper and silver salts to filter toxic gases. Patch test strips are worn on the wrists and shoulders of the suit to detect nerve agents and mustard gas.

Household pesticides are much safer than nerve gases, of course, but the safety directions on the domestic packs I once used are worth contemplating:

> The concentrate is poisonous. Avoid contact with the skin and avoid breathing the mist or vapour. When handling concentrate and preparing spray, use rubber gloves and face shield. If spilled on skin and on completion of each spraying, wash thoroughly with soap and water. Wash contaminated clothing before reuse. Do not eat or smoke while spraying. Secure an emergency supply of Atropine tablets (0.6 mg).

The seller of this product further reassures us with following notice:

> Buyer relies entirely on his own skill or judgement in purchasing this product and in deciding that it may be suitable for the abovementioned purposes' [list of suggested uses].

That is, if you have any problems, speak to my lawyer.

I was cleaning up the syringe in water after treatment of the tree. The washings went onto the ground where they would quickly be destroyed, rather than down the drain. As I put the small bottle of Rogor back in the poisons cupboard, I thought to myself, there really is only a very thin line between war on our own species and war on other species. Our biochemistry is not that different to that of insects, in spite of the enormous structural differences in our life forms. The clothes went into the washing machine and I took my gloves off. The war goes on, with care!

Come on suckers, we'll get you again this year.

FOOD

Can you face science at breakfast?

CHEMICAL THOUGHTS EARLY in the morning: the moment an egg leaves the hen it begins to age. I wonder just how fresh these eggs are? Try some external diagnostics first. Spin an egg on a plate. With your finger stop it momentarily. If it immediately starts to rotate again, it means at least it is not hard-boiled—the contents continue spinning after the shell has been stopped and in turn move the shell again.

Then candle one, which means putting it in front of a light source to give an X-ray view. The yolk tends to drift off-centre with age. Twirling the egg can reveal the quality of the surrounding white, which becomes thinner with age. It also shows the size of the air space, which increases with age as the egg loses water. Fresh eggs sink while older eggs float, broad end higher.

Crack an egg onto a flat plate. The yellowness of the yolk depends on the hen's feed. Often this is boosted by extra beta carotene (the yellow colouring in carrots and tomatoes) extracted from seaweed. Hens fed beta carotene intermittently can show layered-coloured yolks (but the shell colour depends only on the hen breed).

The white of the egg is a protein called albumen. An egg 'breathes' by giving off carbon dioxide and this raises its pH level. The yolk goes from from 6.0 to 6.6, while the albumen goes from 7.7 to 9.2, and sometimes even higher.

Eggs used to be preserved by coating them with sodium silicate (waterglass) or mineral oil. This slowed the egg's breathing and they lived longer. Some commercial producers still do this today.

pHenomenon

The pH level is a measure of how acid a water solution is. A pH of 7 is neutral, while lower values are acidic and higher values are alkaline. Incidentally, egg albumen and baking soda are the only common alkaline ingredients found in the kitchen, the rest are acidic.

Higher pH causes a higher charge on the protein surface. This creates more repulsion between protein molecules. More repulsion causes a flatter and runnier egg.

The albumen (egg white protein) immediately surrounding the yolk is thick, viscous and raised high. Initially, it constitutes about half the egg-white total. With age, there is less of this thick albumen and more of the flatter, runnier kind. The membrane surrounding the yolk also weakens and breaks more easily with age. Egg quality is therefore defined in terms of albumen thickness and yolk (vertical) roundness. Age does not affect nutrition all that much but does affect cooking and baking quality.

The US Centre for Disease Control has issued warnings over the past decade about the dangers of *Salmonella enteritidis* infection from eggs which are raw or lightly cooked. This bacteria causes diarrhoea or worse (arthritis or colon perforation).

According to an article in *The Economist* (4 July 1998), in 1994, egg-contaminated ice-cream caused illness in 224 000 people in the United States (across four States). The risk has increased through industrialisation of egg production whereby hens lack generic variety and conditions may lead to feed contamination and cross infection. Washing the egg removes the natural protective film on the shell allowing contaminated washing water to infect it.

If you put a whole egg into the microwave it will explode. But poaching is fine! Microwaves heat some materials but not others. They heat water very readily but not polythene or glass. They heat fat to a much lesser extent than water.

The plus/minus charge on the microwave needs a plus/minus

Hot air talk about greenhouses

Real greenhouses don't heat up because of the greenhouse effect. If they did then glass sheets would work much better than sheets of plastic, which allow infra-red radiation to pass through much more readily than glass. Salt, which is very transparent to infra-red, also works just as well. The real answer is as follows.

Sunlight heats the ground and plant surface, which in turn heats the air in contact. This air is mechanically trapped by any enclosed transparent sheets and prevented from dispersing by convection.

However, for the atmospheric effect, the technical description (in terms of absorption of infra-red radiation by some components of the atmosphere) greenhouse gasses is correct. It just doesn't apply to greenhouses!

charge on the molecules of the substance to be heated in order to be able to hand over energy efficiently. It's exactly the same process that causes the atmospheric greenhouse effect. While infrared waves are longer and light waves are shorter than microwaves, the theory is the same. Oxygen and nitrogen molecules in the air don't have plus/minus charges and don't take energy from sunlight. Carbon dioxide, methane and chlorofluorocarbon (CFC) molecules do have plus/minus charges and do absorb radiation and heat up.

Microwave ovens have a metal gauze lining the window to stop the microwaves coming out. (They can't get through the metal casing anyway.) Why can we afford to leave spaces in the metal gauze?

Well again, the best explanation comes from looking at the same sort of waves but longer. When you drive your car into a tunnel, you find that the car radio fades out. The radio waves are much longer than microwaves, so a tunnel acts as a 'gauze' for them, and stops them (except where the authorities have put boosters in the tunnel!). AM uses longer waves than FM and its signals can go in a bit deeper. (The tunnels aren't metal but usually have metal reinforcing in the concrete, and anyway, wet soil behaves much the same way.)

Fun with flour

Add water to wheat flour to make dough. Dough is glutinous because of a protein called gluten. The elastic behaviour occurs for the same reason as in vulcanised rubber, springy hair and wool—S–S bonds. Disable this 'protein with the springs' by adding salt and make play dough, which is still mouldable—another protein still acts as a plasticiser but the spring is gone. Bake in a low oven (100°C) to set and then paint.

How fast does a smell travel?

Finally, if you haven't bothered to get out of bed and are waiting to be served breakfast, then the following scenario might interest you. You are lying in bed sipping a fragrant Lavazza, and there is suddenly a yell from the kitchen at the other end of the house. The smell of burnt toast seems to arrive 'immediately' with the yell . . . Strange, because in still air, smoke (from say a fire or cigarette) hardly moves sideways much at all.

The molecules in air move very fast, averaging around 1740 kilometres per hour (1000 mph) for oxygen, a bit slower for the heavier burnt aroma molecules. But because they are pretty crowded they bump into each other a lot and the average distance between collisions is only one ten-thousandth of a millimetre! So the bulk of molecules in still air hardly moves at all, but the very, very small fraction of an enormous number that get a reasonably clear run zoom across the house at around the speed of sound. But then sound is transmitted by waves caused by air molecules bumping into each other, so I guess it is not so surprising that both signals come through at roughly the same time.

Yes I know. With explanations like that you are glad you stayed in bed and don't need to bother.

Where Marge got her name

On some tubs of polyunsaturated margarine sitting on our breakfast tables will be written the content of *linoleic acid,* one of the polyunsaturated fatty acids we eat in the hope of reducing our chance of cholesterol depositing in our arteries (with a faint suspicion of increasing the risk of cancer!). Vegetable seeds are the source of these oils—linseed oil is a good source, although it is not used for food. Can we see a connection between the words *linseed* and *linoleic*? Another link is with the word *linoleum*. Good old 'lino' was made by pouring linseed oil over hessian (with a few rosins thrown in) and allowing it to harden in air (like putty and oil paints, also made from linseed oil). Today we use plastics like PVC and, until very recently, asbestos matting. From lino we make linotile and linotype.

What about the *linen* cupboard? Unless you have very expensive tastes you should really call it a cotton cupboard. Linen comes from the flax plant (genus *Linum*) whose seeds are linseeds! And as for *lint*? These are just the linen (cotton) scrapings.

And as for Marge, well her name came from margaric acid...

When do you reach
flashpoint?

A FLASH IN the pan. You've got a steak in the griller and the vapourised fat hits the hot grill. Or you are frying on the hotplate and the fuming oil drifts down towards the hotplate. Why is there sometimes (but not always) a sudden flash of fire?

They say (don't try it) you can put out a burning cigarette in a full can of petrol (mostly!)—but drop it into a petrol can 'emptied' of its liquid contents and you're almost guaranteed of an almighty explosion. When and why are flammable liquids and their vapours sometimes safe and other times dangerous?

The fact is that a mixture of fuel and air is only explosive over a limited range of fuel–air mixtures. If there is too little fuel it won't burn. But also if there is too much fuel and too little air, it won't burn either.

These upper and lower limits are called the flammability or explosion limits. Take a typical component of petrol and LPG, n-pentane. Pentane will only burn in air when the percent by volume of pentane is between 1.5 and 7.5. Apply a spark or flame to mixtures with higher and lower pentane content and no burning or explosion takes place.

Methyl ether is replacing CFCs in some aerosol propellants. But the limits of explosive mixtures are much wider for ethers than for hydrocarbons, ranging from 2 to 48 per cent. Chlorofluorocarbons are non-flammable and so were greeted with joy when introduced into domestic products. But now we know they destroy the ozone layer.

Even more extreme are mixtures of hydrogen and air, which will burn or explode in the range of 4 to 74 per cent of

Explosion limits of petrol

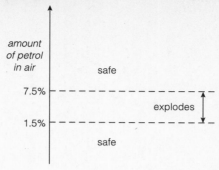

hydrogen, which is why the hydrogen-filled airship *Hindenberg* exploded on its maiden trip to the United States. The limits for acetylene are greater still at 2.5 to 80 per cent.

So now we know there is a range of mixtures fuel and air must be in to be set off by a spark or flame.

The temperature at which enough vapour is given off to sustain burning is called the 'flash point' for that substance, that is the temperature at which a liquid will produce enough vapour to reach the lower explosion/burning limit.

The flash point for petrol is below 0°C so it is easy to reach a mixture in air above the lower limit, which is what a car engine depends on. Petrol left in a sealed container produces vapour above the upper limit so it will only start to burn when it comes in contact with extra air outside the container which dilutes the vapour sufficiently.

In kerosene pressure (hurricane) lamps and stoves (blow torches etc), methylated spirits (alcohol) is initially lit in a cup around the kero burner. The flash point for meths is 13°C, so it is easy to heat and light with a match. On cold days some warming with a match is needed. The heat from the burning meths then warms up the kerosene to above its flash point (46°C). When this is reached the kerosene will sustain the amount of vapour to continue to burn on its own.

So why is it possible to directly light kero lamps and heaters with wicks?

A wick is made from fibrous or spongy material which behaves like a large number of very thin tubes. Wicks suck up liquid spontaneously (by capillary action). On emerging, the liquid covers a large surface which exposes it to more air and

Strike it lucky

A farmer in New South Wales owes his life to explosion limits. The oil tank to his heater was filled with petrol by mistake. When his oil heater went out, he kept trying to light it with a match. Luckily the vapours were too concentrated otherwise he would have blown himself up.

also allows it to evaporate faster to form vapour. So the heat of a match is sufficient to heat the kerosene in a wick to above its flash point, even if it is insufficient to heat the bulk liquid.

Try lighting a candle without a wick (or one that is too short or lying flat). It is very difficult. Candle wicks are also designed to curl over at the top and burn off at the edge of the flame. So wick snuffers to cut off wicks as the candle recedes are no longer needed.

If mineral turpentine (flash point 32°C) from a paint clean-up is soaked up into a rag, the rag will act as a wick. A match can then be sufficient to cause ignition.

Product mixing (contamination) can greatly change the flash point. A mere 1 per cent petrol added to home heating oil (diesel—flash point 69°C) lowers the flash point to about 52°C. This would bring the oil well below the safety limit specified by law of 65.5°C.

Do you always need a flash or spark to start a fire or will a substance spontaneously combust just from heating up or contacting something hot? Well, diesel engines work just that way. The fuel and air are heated by compression through the piston. The fuel spontaneously combusts when it gets hot enough. No spark is needed.

The temperature of self-start burning is called the auto-ignition temperature. For kerosene it is 250°C. For petrol it varies but even the maximum of 430°C is well within the range of a stove hotplate or incandescent light globe (if broken when on), a quality many an arsonist has explored. Petrol engines with coked-up cylinders can have carbon glowing after ignition and this can cause auto-ignition of the next charge of petrol and air (called dieselling). Fat vapour from a steak can catch fire on a hot griller element!

Many an industrial and domestic accident has started this way, including the disastrous fire aboard the HMAS *Westralian* in early 1998, when a broken fuel line allowed fuel to spill onto hot piping.

The explosion of TWA flight 800 off Long Island, USA, in July 1996 killed 230 people and is thought to have been caused by the ignition of jet fuel in one of the tanks. It has been proposed to cool fuel to 1°C or below before it is pumped into an aircraft to keep it out of the flammability range for some hours (See *New Scientist* 25 September 1999).

Bitumen is a good example of a substance with an auto-ignition point (260°C) not much higher than the temperatures at which it is prepared and used. Heated liquid bitumen (in refineries) must be kept in closed containers under a layer of steam, otherwise it could burst into flames.

Unsaturated oils are subject to auto-oxidation, which leads to peroxides that degrade the molecule to a complex mixture of volatile aldehydes, ketones and acids—called rancidity. Because of natural anti-oxidants, vegetable oils are more resistant to auto-oxidation. Waste or rags containing unsaturated oils can spontaneously combust in the presence of air. Just look at the warning on containers of boiled linseed oil. With poor ventilation the temperature can rise and increase the rate of oxidation, eventually leading to flames.

Spontaneous combustion of people has often been reported but never substantiated, but in the early 1900s, a New Zealand Royal Commission investigated wool bales dispatched by ship to London that arrived charred in the centre and totally ruined.

This self-heating of wool was accentuated by the New Zealand practice of slaughtering lambs for meat and then extracting the wool from the pelt to produce 'slipe wool', in contrast to the Australian practice of shearing live sheep. Water and grease attached to the wool along with some of the chemicals used in obtaining the wool from the pelt accelerated the process of combustion.

The fibre protein in wool causes it to become fluid in the early stages of self-heating, which leads to fusion of the sample in the hottest part, in the centre where oxygen is excluded. There it chars, discolouring further out, with the outside untouched. Wool in clothing needs a generous supply of air to burn outright and skiers at high altitude find that wool is safe because the lower level of oxygen will not sustain a flame in wool. Cotton being cellulose behaves more like paper and requires flame retardants to protect it. The early retardants were found to be carcinogenic and had to be removed from sale.

The pale light of the will-o'-the-wisp seen over marshland or burning compost piles is caused by the ignition of methane triggered by the spontaneous combustion of diphosphane when it meets air. Diphosphane is produced bacterially.

So there is a bit more to this chemical story than just a flash in the pan.

Distilling the essence—
why use steam?

BLINDFOLDED AND WITH your nostrils pegged, you can't tell much difference between biting into an apple and biting into a peeled potato. Your taste is actually mostly smell. With a heavy cold and blocked nose, you have probably realised this. What you may not appreciate is that there is often a need for water to evaporate with the aroma molecules in order to bring them to your nose.

Chemicals which boil at high temperatures and would not normally evaporate much on their own will co-distil with water in a process called steam distillation. The aroma of a hot cup of tea or coffee is brought to you courtesy of the steam.

Eucalyptus and other lovely essential oils (named 'essential' in the sense that they have an essence) would char to something horrible if the leaves were heated to boil off the oils directly. This would need temperatures ranging from 200°C to 300°C. By using steam to co-distil, the temperature never reaches beyond 100°C and protects the oils. You never throw lavender oil directly onto sauna coals. Mixing it with water prevents charring.

The attractive aroma released from frying in oil is carried to your nose by water. Some natural anti-oxidant or additives in the oil also distil off—so cooking oils shouldn't be reused very often. High levels of natural anti-oxidant vitamin E in cooking oil are better than synthetic anti-oxidants because the natural molecule comes with a long molecular chain. This holds it back in the oil and delays the steam dragging it out of the oil.

Other high boiling-point chemicals that won't move without water nevertheless have lasting environmental consequences. For example, POPs (persistent organic pollutants), like DDT and PCB (polychlorinated biphenyl) or HCB (hexachlorobenzene), are organic molecules (often chlorinated), which were once widely used in agriculture and industry. They are not biodegraded (which is why they were chosen), and have very high boiling points. So if they don't evaporate, how come they have spread right around the globe to contaminate pristine places like Antarctica?

The same way as eucalyptus. Once they enter rivers and the ocean they can co-evaporate with the water, enter the atmosphere, and then float off around the globe.

Winter often means lighting up the log fire. Wood contains an awful lot of natural chemicals and they become more awful when heated and charred. Luckily they have high boiling points and mostly burn close to the red hot wood surface. However, if you are naughty and use green or wet timber, the extra water provides perfect conditions for the nasties to steam-distil off and rise up the flue before being burnt. They either pollute the neighbourhood or condense in your flue, build up and later catch fire. Or both.

These toxic, carcinogenic, allergenic molecules rise through your chimney and can get stuck under an early morning atmospheric inversion layer. This ensures they stay down low where the whole valley can breathe them in. They are nowhere near as pleasant as the aroma from a steaming cuppa but the same chemistry applies—steam distillation.

Forget the fags—cooking oil fumes can give you cancer!

RECEIVED AN e-mail from a bloke working long hours in a fish and chip shop who was worried about his health being affected by the continuous heavy oil fumes in the shop. I passed this on to Worksafe Australia. As part of its review of the matter, Worksafe did a computer literature search and passed me back the print-outs. Worrying.

Not worrying from the point of view of the food, mind you, but from that of inhaling the fumes. Chemical extraction of the condensed fumes reveals an array of cancer-causing substances in significant concentration. That is not a surprise. Heating most organic matter to cooking temperatures for hours on end will do that. Biological studies also show that the fume condensates cause significant genetic mutations in an array of standard short-term tests. That also is not new. What is new is a link with lung cancer.

Epidemiological studies in Taiwan show that lung cancer in women is the leading cause of cancer deaths in Taiwan. But most Chinese women are non-smokers. Worldwide non-smokers mostly have very little incidence of primary lung cancer; in those who do, it is often attributed to indoor exposure to radioactive radon gas from rock. In the study 117 Taiwanese women suffering from lung cancer (including 106 non-smokers) were interviewed, and compared with the same number of individually matched hospital controls. Analysis indicated that cooking oil fumes in kitchens without extractors over a significant period of years was a major factor.

Similar results in bigger studies have been found in Hong Kong,

Singapore and Hawaii. Fascinatingly, the Hong Kong studies showed that incense burning produces high levels of indoor nitrogen oxides and carcinogens. But smoking women had a highly significant reduction in lung cancer if they regularly burnt incense. Incense burning had no positive effect on non-smokers. So incense is good for you, eh?

Well, it would appear that women who are better off burn incense and they tend to have much better diets. The women who cooked for long periods (25 years or more) and who had higher rates of lung cancer, on the other hand, tended to be not very well off and had poor diets. Good diet (lots of fresh fruit and vegetables) appears to be a major compounding factor that causes a small reduction in the incidence of lung cancer in smokers. The positive influence of incense was spurious.

Long-term inhaling of high levels of oil fumes, be it from cooking, cars or poorly tuned boilers, or from leaking hydraulics inside aircraft cabins, is all bad news. The bloke from the fish and chip shop changed his e-mail (or died!) and can't be reached, but he was right to be worried. Perhaps Worksafe will take the matter further with State health inspectors. For all of us, it is a good lesson on how careful you need to be when attempting to relate cause and effect, and how much of health is improved by very simple, long-known, sensible, eating habits.

Some will remain incensed!

Guess why bananas gassed in their pyjamas taste ghastly?

DURING 19TH CENTURY winters in Europe, people were reluctant to put flowers and plants in rooms with (coal) gas fires because they didn't seem to last. In the middle of the summer of 1864 it was noted that trees near leaking gas mains shed their leaves. In 1910 farmers in the Caribbean Islands found their bananas ripened sooner when stored next to oranges. In 1912 a Californian grocer found that green citrus fruit turned yellow near a kerosene stove, but unfortunately they did not ripen. Car exhausts did the same to the citrus fruit in Sydney's street fruit vendor stalls.

What was (and is) going on?

We now know that the very simple gas ethylene (two carbons, four hydrogens, C_2H_4, from which polythene plastic is made) is a natural ripening hormone. It works at the incredibly low level of around 1 part per million.

Plants that exhibit this energetic ethylene-induced ripening are called climacteric. These include mangoes, pears, nectarines, peaches, avocados, pawpaws and tomatoes. Apples produce the gas over a long period (except Granny Smiths and Fuji). Bananas also produce it, while passionfruits produce most gas of all but in a short burst. Bruising causes excess ethylene release and hence 'one rotten apple can spoil the whole barrow'.

On ripening, green chlorophyll disappears and other colours previously masked show through. Apples turn red and bananas turn yellow. Release of ethylene by an apple in your refrigerator can cause the bright green head of broccoli to turn yellow as well.

Banana growers carefully control this ethylene ripening process. Bananas are picked green and stored cold or in bags with ethylene-removing compounds. They are then 'ripened' a few days prior to sale by gassing them. However, a naturally ripening banana converts 25 per cent starch into 20 per cent sugar leaving 1 per cent starch (the loss is used for respiration). Bad timing of gassing leaves the fruit with a starchy taste.

You can use one fruit to ripen another by storing them together in a paper bag. Don't use plastic because carbon dioxide from the 'breathing' fruit accumulates and this slows down ripening. Commercial use is made of this effect by packing green fruit in carbon dioxide to delay ripening.

Want to try an interesting experiment? Pea seedlings grown in the dark are tall and slender but exposed to a trace of ethylene their stems become short and curly. You might even be able to use a pea to sniff out a ripe banana or leaking gas pipe.

Anti-what? It can't be the oxygen we breathe!

ONCE UPON A time (3.8 billion years ago) the earth's atmosphere had no oxygen at all. It was mainly carbon dioxide.

Life forms called autotrophs (self-feeders) obtained energy by various chemical means that are used much more rarely today. Other organisms—heterotrophs—lived by eating these.

The earth was hot because of a greenhouse effect, but not of course green! This state of affairs persisted for a long time. Then disaster occurred. Photosynthesis started and oxygen appeared.

Finally, nearly all the carbon dioxide was replaced with oxygen, to become 20 per cent of the current total atmosphere.

The carbon from the carbon dioxide gas was fixed carbon in fossil fuel deposits and oceanic-derived carbonates (limestones). If all the carbonates were calcined, like on hot Venus, we would also have 60 atmospheres' pressure of carbon dioxide (again).

As oxygen appeared in the environment, organisms were faced with a choice—to specialise in an environment without oxygen (anoxic) or to adapt to oxygen environments (oxic). Generally speaking, anaerobes chose anoxic safety at the cost of biological innovation and were condemned to small size. (Some deep-sea anaerobes are quite large—for example, the tube worm *riftia* which lives around black smokers— but that is because of a unique association between the deep sea anaerobes and sulfur-metabolising bacteria.) On land, the original dominant anaerobes today survive in niches like bogs and swamps. They are also found in fermentation processes, some as disease microbes (e.g. botulism).

Years	Oxygen levels
2.5 billion years ago	0.3% of present oxygen levels
2 billion years ago	about 1% of present oxygen levels
1 billion years ago	about 2% of present oxygen levels
0.65 billion years ago	about 10% of present oxygen levels

Lavoisier, the discoverer of the role of oxygen in combustion, found that guinea pigs soon died when kept enclosed in pure oxygen, long before the gas had run out. He thought it was the build up of carbon dioxide they breathed out that killed them, but other workers soon found that to include soda to absorb and remove the carbon dioxide made no difference. Oxygen *is* poisonous. Premature babies once treated with high concentrations of oxygen developed retinal detachment and blindness.

Oxygen attacks polyunsaturated oils and fats and forms what are called peroxides. Peroxides have an attached oxygen atom on the end of the molecule carrying a single electron. Any such an arrangement with a single electron is called a free radical. Unlike the usual paired electrons bonding atoms in molecules, these free radicals with their single electrons are chemically very reactive because the single electron is looking for another electron with which to form a pair.

An example of peroxide formation and the resulting reactivity is seen in the effect of air on (poly)unsaturated oils like canola, sunflower and linseed. Oxygen in the air slowly gives the surface of exposed oil a solid skin. The process continues downwards until the oil finally turns into a gluggy gell. Linseed oil based paints and varnishes make use of this effect to turn the liquid paint into a solid film. Unfortunately, on a painted surface the process continues below the skin so that the paint finally disintegrates and peels off. The linseed oil is often boiled beforehand to initiate the peroxidation and rags soaked in such oil can spontaneously ignite from overfast peroxidation (p. 57). However, it is not true that people who eat too much linseed bread spontaneously combust when they die.

Free radicals formed from oxygen and fats can also attack the sulfur-hydrogen (SH) groups of the proteins in essential body enzymes. They destroy the peptide glutathione (important as a natural anti-oxidant), and attack cell membranes. Nasty buggers.

Anaerobic biomass

Anaerobes still form a substantial proportion of the world's biomass because the sediment at the bottom of all bodies of water contains an oxygen free layer that may be metres deep and is occupied by a whole host of small, interesting organisms. When you consider how much of the world is covered by water you can see that the volume of this biomass is enormous. In water columns, an oxygen minimum zone is found between 100 and 1000 metres in depth. Some water bodies like the Black Sea are anaerobic.

Vertebrates in particular used oxygen as a weapon. Their cellular immune system works by generating oxygen-derived free radicals in the presence of attacking organisms and using it to destroy invading cell membranes. We do the same when we use hydrogen peroxide as a disinfectant.

Both plants and animals have developed anti-oxidants for dealing with oxygen generated free radicals turning up in the wrong places. We also obtain additional help by eating lots of fresh fruit and vegetables and using their anti-oxidants, the flavonoids or polyphenols.

Flavonoids are a huge group of related chemicals. About 4000 have been identified but there are many possibilities because they can combine in various ways to form new ones. They include plant colours—anthocyanins—(except for green chlorophyll) and chemicals such as vitamin E. Within this group are also the catechins found in cocoa and thus in *real* chocolate. Dark cocoa-based chocolate contains about 50 milligrams per 100 grams, while black tea has around 14 milligrams per 100 millilitres (*Canberra Times*, 8 August 1999).

Derived from the flavonoids (and part of the same group) are the very closely related tannins or polyphenols. High levels of these are found in tea and red wine. They are also extracted from tree barks and used for natural tanning of hides.

There are lots of herbal extracts on the market claiming anti-oxidant action. Tannins are great anti-oxidants (neutralising free radicals), and extracts of red wine, black olives, grape seeds, red clover and pine bark are all marketed as new elixirs for a long life.

Tannins are interesting in other ways

Adding milk to tea causes a reaction between milk protein (casein) and the tannins in tea, making the brew less astringent. The tannins in barley react with proteins to give home brews a haze. This can be 'clarified' by adding more protein (often gelatine).

The process of tanning, whereby skins are turned into leather, was traditionally done using (vegetable) tannins from plants like wattle. The skin protein (collagen) reacts with tannin making it unattractive as a food for microbes.

Sun-tanning doesn't use any tannins, but the effect is the same, turning skin into leather, finally making it unattractive to more than just microbes.

I prefer wine as my major source of these materials.

> O for a beaker full of the warm South,
> Full of the true, the blushful Hippocrene,
> With beaded bubbles winking at the brim,
> and purple-stainèd mouth;
> That I might drink, and leave the world unseen,
> And with thee fade away into the forest dim

J. Keats, 'Ode to a Nightingale', *A Book of Poetry*

This stanza illustrates one property of wine pigments: they act as acid base indicators. The red colouring in the acid wine turns purple on the lips—lips tend to be almost neutral in pH.

The taste of tannin (polymeric polyphenols) is one of the characteristics of a good red wine. The tannins come from the grapes skins which go into the fermentation broth for red wines (from both red or white grapes).

Different tannins come from the oak in which the wines may be matured. As traditional storage in oak is expensive, oak chips in stainless steel barrels are sometimes substituted. However, it is difficult to control the amount of tannin extracted from the chips and some wines taste 'oaky' instead of 'okay'. Tannins are found in many plants and trees. Chestnuts provide a quick and easy source of soluble extract, which then allows controlled addition to the fermentation vats. Chestnut and beech also provide good barrel material.

Red wines change colour with age because these anti-oxidant tannins react with with oxygen causing the tannins to aggregate. After the first year the colour improves. With longer storage the polymers get bigger, the colour becomes rubier through to plum to brick red. These natural anti-oxidants help protect the other flavour components and contribute to the observation that red wines are more tolerant of air than white. Indeed, barrel storage allows controlled oxygen uptake. In the bottle further chemical changes take place and eventually a brown sediment hails the end of a wine.

Persimmon is a fruit which can be very astringent. This makes it hard to swallow because the tannins it contains precipitate mucins, proteins in the saliva that would normally be able to act as lubricants for swallowing.

And that's also why tannins give wine and tea their bite; they actually tan your tongue.

And good for your heart? Evidence suggests it is the moderate alcohol intake that is important. (See 'The French Paradox' pp. 8–9.)

Which pills of vitamin E, if any?

FOR THE FIRST few days after we die, we absorb oxygen faster than we ever did when we were alive and breathing!

The reason is that the anti-oxidant protection for our fats is now inoperative, and bacteria ensure that we go off like a bucket of prawns in the sun. In spite of occasional reports of the spontaneous combustion of dead bodies, the process usually doesn't go as far as this!

Two vitamins act as anti-oxidant and protect our body. Vitamin C (ascorbic acid), protects our watery bits while vitamin E (a mixture of alpha, beta, gamma and delta-tocopherol), protects the fatty bits. These two vitamins reinforce one another.

The biological activity of both natural and synthetic vitamin E supplements is tested by feeding female rats a diet free of any vitamin E for some months. If impregnated by males, the resulting foetuses produced all die and are reabsorbed by the female. The activity of natural and synthetic vitamin E is tested by feeding controlled amounts of vitamin E to the vitamin deprived females to see to what extent the reabsorption is prevented.

In the words of one (liberated) researcher 'men are not just big rats'. The rat is not a good indicator.

The fat protective vitamin E molecule looks a bit like a tadpole. It has a business head which is a phenol anti-oxidant. To this is attached a tail that anchors the molecule into cell membranes.

When a plant produces vitamin E it adds one group of atoms

Alpha tocopherol—vitamin E

antioxidant business end

anchor chain with three
geometry choices

α, β, γ, δ
variation in the
add ons

at a time. Occasionally there is a choice in the orientation of the added group. This is a bit like choosing a left or right hand. It makes no difference to the atomic connections (and thus little to chemical behaviour), but it does affect the geometric shape (and thus its biological activity). There are three such choices in the tail of vitamin E and therefore eight possible final geometries (2x2x2). Of these eight, the plant chooses only one. The 'business end' of the molecule is not always complete and that is why we have four varieties called alpha, beta, gamma and delta tocopherol.

However, back at the health store, the vitamin E supplements on sale are often cheap and synthetic. The chemist's brew contains all eight choices in equal amounts (instead of the one the plant has selected) and sticks to alpha for the business head (and forgets about the beta, gamma and delta options). The synthetic vitamin is labelled 'dl-alpha tocopherol'. Where 'd' (*dextro*, right) and 'l' (*laevo*, left), tell that the chemist has mixed the three right and left choices at random for every molecule as it is synthesised.

Separating chemicals that differ only in this left/right choice is horrendously difficult and thus expensive. Natural vitamin E, 'd-alpha tocopherol', is extracted and purified from a biproduct of plant oil production along with other salable items like fatty acids and phytosterols. Soya, corn, rapeseed, sunflower and cottonseed oils are used.

The question is, what is the effect on us of having a synthetic mixture instead of nature's choice?

Some animal research has suggested that the natural vitamin

was 1.36 times as potent as the synthetic mix. However, as the liver can detect a non-plant molecule at one of three points of choice and throw it out, this would suggest the natural vitamin is at least twice as potent as the synthetic version. There is also evidence that there is a second choice spot somewhere else in our body where ring-ins are checked and again rejected. If proven, this would up the effectiveness ratio of natural to synthetic to four times. Some foods like soya beans have gamma tocopherol as the major vitamin E component, but our livers toss it out even though it does quite a good job as an anti-oxidant.

Vitamine E in a bottle is provided as a derivative called an ester, a temporary chemical link to make it stable in the bottle. This link is broken in the small intestine to release the actual vitamin. Animal research once suggested that this synthetic ester was twice as potent as the natural, but this never made chemical sense and has since been shown to be false.

Vitamine E deficiency is very rare except in certain disease states. Supplements may have a role in some disease prevention, but it would seem the best (and cheapest) bet is to stay with a wide variety of whole foods, fresh and in season.

And rats have turned out to be poor models for humans.

Source

Based in part on a recent lecture at the ANU by chemistry Professor Keith Ingold of the University of Toronto, Canada and on information supplied by Faulding Health Care.

Veggie out—before they get you first!

IF BUTCHERS AND restaurants had to play videos for customers depicting scenes of abbatoirs in action, meat consumption would drop precipitously. Vegetarians would gloat. But *those* nasty people eat *live* plants at their prime of life, sometimes even ripping out their tender young seeds in which mother has placed all her hope for the future. And the vegos eat them with relish.

But plants *want* us to eat them, don't they? No bloody way. Let us look at one plant chemical warfare project. Howard Bradbury, a retired ANU chemist, yarns about a Nigerian cassava that is so deadly it is called 'chop and die'. Not so funny in a struggling developing country.

The origin of cassava (tapioca) has been traced to the southern border of the Amazon River basin in Brazil, using DNA fingerprints to work out its geneology. There seem to be thousands of different varieties. In Brazil, every little village has its own varieties. There are bitter ones, sweet ones, even ones used as baby food.

Cassava was introduced to Africa by the Portuguese more than 300 years ago, and today is the primary carbohydrate source in sub-Saharan Africa. It is a drought-resistant crop valued for its tubers, which grows in poor soils and it feeds at least 600 million people in both the wet and dry tropics. However, the plant produces a cyanogenic glucoside. Almonds and other stone fruit kernels have non-toxic levels of such glycosides as well. Bitterness is an indication of their levels. Glycosides are sugar-based complexes which keep a poison

locked up. Our bodies use the same lock-up trick when detoxifying some poisons we encounter internally. But when the plant
cells are damaged by predators (insect and human), the plants
release an enzyme which breaks down the glycoside, releasing
hydrogen cyanide in toxic amounts—chemical warfare the
subtlety of which we have yet to match.

Indigenous South Americans learnt to avoid poisoning themselves by spitting into batches of ground tubers; the saliva
introduces bacteria and fungi, which activate a detoxifying
enzyme. It is speculated that starvation indirectly led to these
culinary rituals; starving people may have found that, having once
spat out the bitter cassava tubers, then trying them desperately
again much later, the bitter taste had lessened. Present-day
villagers accomplish the same thing by depositing freshly dug
cassava tubers into a community pond; micro-organisms in the
water degrade the cyanide.

In Africa, peeled cassava roots are usually cut end to end
and heaped to ferment followed by drying in the sun (or just
dried) for seven days. This allows the detoxifying enzyme to do
its deadly deed, but also allows the cyanide to disperse. The
dried plant is pounded in a wooden mortar and pestle and sieved
to produce a flour.

Australian Aborigines faced a similar problem when utilising
local cycads as a source of flour. The poisonous principal is
methylazoxymethanol—cyanide was not at issue. According to
the region, various methods were used to detoxify them including leaching with running water, fermentation in pits or
roasting. Cycads were often ground into flour and baked as
loaves. Captain Cook's crew saw the food but not the kitchen
and almost died when they thought they would prepare it
themselves.

By adapting a colour reaction process discovered in 1859 for
detecting cyanide, Howard Bradbury developed a kit for testing
cassava in developing countries. The kit uses a paper strip
dipped in a solution of yellow picric acid (tri-nitrophenol—an
explosive when dry), which turns brown in the presence of
cyanide. This has trialled successfully.

Apart from the occasional death and more frequent acute
intoxication by cyanide poisoning, an estimated 10 000 people
in Africa suffer from sudden irreversible paralysis of the legs
(called konzo) caused by chronic sub-lethal cyanide poisoning.

This occurs most frequently when there is little time to process cassava properly—like in times of drought and war—not uncommon in the region.

I think I'll stick to meat.

What's so special
about coffee?

IN 1732 J.S. BACH wrote the 'Coffee Cantata' to accompany lyrics that included, 'Hail, hail to thee coffee; Hail, hail best of blisses'. But around the same time, convinced that coffee was poisonous, King Gustav III of Sweden sentenced a murderer to death by the drinking of one cup of coffee a day. He pardoned another murderer but required him to drink one cup of tea per day. Two physicians were appointed to follow up the cases and record the deaths. The result of this exemplary scientific experiment was as follows: the doctors died first, followed by Gustav, who was murdered; the tea drinker succumbed later at the age of 83, and the condemned man survived them all.

Unfiltered coffee appears to raise blood cholesterol levels. The main culprit seems to be cafestol, found in oil droplets that float on the surface of the brew and suspended in the coffee bean grinds. Filtering removes nearly all the cafestol but it is abundant in Scandinavian-style boiled coffee and other turbid types like Turkish, French press and espresso. Experiments with 8 grams of fine coffee grinds per day (fed to volunteers in a caramel-flavoured dairy dessert) raised cholesterol levels after three weeks on average by 25 milligrams per 100 millilitres (US measure), or 0.65 millimoles per litre (European/Australian measure) compared with a control group whose levels remained the same. The amount of 8 grams is equivalent to about 1.5 litres of Turkish coffee per day (*Consumer Reports on Health*, February 1996).

Coffee smells darned good, courtesy of steam distillation of the essences (see p. 59). The most disappointing part is that so often it smells better than it tastes. Good coffee is a little bitter but it should be rich and full. Grinders Coffee House is a Melbourne favourite. Lavazza, Geovese, Belaroma, Mocopan and, for something more bitter, Vittoria, are all good. The most important thing with all these brands is that the coffee comes from one type of bean, the arabica. The reason coffee varies so much is only partly due to the coffee bean. Other things that make the difference are the machine, the freshness and the operator. Take a good brand of coffee, then grind it without it getting too hot—otherwise the aroma will volatilise. Buy often and in small amounts; store airtight and preferably in a freezer on opening.

Espresso machines make the richest textured coffee and actually release less caffeine than dripolators. Plungers use a coarser grind and make a less complex coffee.

Coffee is consumed in one form or another by about one-third of the world's population. The two most important commercial varieties are *Coffea robusta* and *Coffea arabica*. *Coffee robusta*, grown in West Africa and Indonesia, has a higher caffeine content. *Coffee arabica*, grown in East Africa, Central and South America, the Caribbean and New Guinea, yields a stronger flavour. Blending and roasting change the character of the product considerably.

Instant coffee was introduced to Australia by the US armed forces in 1938, and it is now the most widely used form of coffee here. Australian food regulations set a minimum level of 3 per cent for caffeine in instant coffee, which requires a greater use of the milder *C. robusta* beans.

Decaffeinated coffee has a longer Australian history, having been introduced by the German firm Kaffee HAG in the early 1900s, but has only now attracted a loyal and growing market. There was concern about the safety of the solvent, trichlorethylene, used to extract the caffeine from coffee. However, the safer trichlorethane and liquid carbon dioxide are now used.

Worldwide consumption of caffeine has been estimated at 120 000 tonnes per annum, which works out at 70 milligrams per person per day. Approximately 54 per cent of this is from coffee, 43 per cent from tea and 3 per cent from other sources. In spite of the image of the United States as a heavy coffee-consuming country, Scandinavians consume almost three times as much caffeine from coffee (340 mg/day) as Americans, while the British match the Scandinavians in their caffeine intake from tea (320 mg/day). Only the United States and Canada show significant caffeine intake from soft drinks (35 and 16 mg/day respectively). Caffeine is allowed in non-cola drinks in these countries (but not in Australia). The total caffeine intakes of United States and Canada (211 and 238 mg/day respectively) is well below that of Sweden (425 mg/day) and Britain (444 mg/day). The estimated level of consumption of caffeine in Australia is 240 milligrams per day from all sources.

In addition to caffeine, tea contains about 1 milligram per cup of the much more active alkaloid theophylline, while cocoa contains about 250 milligrams per cup of the much less active alkaloid theobromine (which does not contain bromine). Plants store these chemicals in their leaves as a natural insecticide. Tea and coffee grounds are therefore also effective as insecticides or repellents.

Modern medicine makes use of caffeine as a respiratory stimulant and the related theophylline for bronchial asthma (doses for adults are in the 250 mg range). But take care: caffeine and the benzodiazepine drugs (e.g. Valium) counter each others' effects.

There have also been many studies attempting to link coffee with disease. Unfortunately, the many symptoms attributable to excess caffeine are those for which a cup of coffee is often self-prescribed: insomnia, irritability, headache, palpitations, diuresis and diarrhoea. Folklore has it that people vary considerably in their response to caffeine. Some claim to sleep like a log after several cups at night while others find that a single cup causes them to rage into the wee small hours. Closely controlled experiments do not bear these claims out, however, and variables such as long-term intake play a large part in perceived differences to caffeine intake.

The symptoms of caffeine withdrawal are usually mild and seldom last for more than seven days. They usually start within 18 hours and include a diffuse throbbing headache made worse by exercise (like a 'tension' headache).

Caffeine is metabolised in the liver and the half life (the time required to reduce the level in the body to half its initial value) is three to four hours. The metabolising rate is increased by smoking. It is greatly slowed in the later stages of pregnancy, an effect related to endocrine function. It is well established that women automatically reduce their caffeine intake during pregnancy. In fact, the consumption of caffeine, unlike many other drugs, is self-regulating—you stop drinking when you've had enough.

So what if your pots and pans dissolve in the puree?

WHAT ABOUT COOKING with good old-fashioned pots and pans?

Iron

In the good old days they used cast-iron pots. Iron was heavy but conducted heat efficiently and held the heat for some time. It had another advantage; a small amount of iron dissolved in the food becoming a major dietary source, of particular importance in preventing anaemia in menstruating women.

Cooking eggs in iron pots turns the eggs green. This is because the iron dissolved from the pot reacts with the sulfur in the egg white forming (green) iron sulfide. Not a problem, except perhaps aesthetically. We know that there is sulfur in eggs because when they go bad they give off 'rotten egg gas', which is hydrogen sulfide.

Copper

Then came copper. Copper is one of the best conductors of heat. Copper also dissolves slightly in food acids. In small amounts this is not a problem. In fact, beating eggs in a copper bowl produces a wonderfully stable foam because this time the dissolved copper reacts with the egg white and appears to make it a much better stabilising agent for foams. Too much dissolved copper can cause vomiting. This occasionally occurs in (say) freezer trays used for making iceblocks if they have been partially stripped of their tin lining, exposing the underlying copper.

Aluminium

Next came aluminium. Aluminium is light, and on a weight basis, a better conductor than copper. Aluminium does react with acids, so you can clean a pot by boiling rhubarb in it. However, it is not a good idea to then eat the rhubarb if it has been left sitting there for some time because of the high level of dissolved aluminium.

Black spots are sometimes found on the bottom of aluminium pots. This is probably just carbon black or iron left over from the manufacturing process and revealed as the surface dissolves.

As well as reacting with acids, aluminium also reacts with alkalis. The Draino that you pour down a blocked sink consists of aluminium filings and caustic soda. In contact with water the aluminium reacts with the caustic, furiously heats up and releases hydrogen gas (often carrying bits of caustic—so don't breathe it or let it touch your face!).

Aluminium is an unusual metal. It is so very reactive that you could expect it to catch fire in air spontaneously—or at least for mag wheels (aluminium magnesium alloy) to dissolve if a dog lifted its leg and peed on them.

The reason it is nevertheless so stable is because it forms a very stable thin layer of aluminium oxide on the surface, which stops any further corrosion. Aluminium 'rusts' much faster than iron, but the aluminium 'rust' is not crumbly, it stays on as a tough coherent layer—unless the oxide is destroyed by, say, a salt spray. Aluminium is alloyed with a range of other metals like copper for products used near or on the sea to prevent this.

The tough oxide layer of aluminium is enhanced in coloured aluminium products, which are made by a process called 'anodising'. The protective oxide layer is deliberately made thicker by an electrolysing process, at the same time incorporating a pigment.

Untarnishing silver

A milder reaction of the Draino type is used for cleaning tarnished silverware (including silver plate).

Your tarnished silver has formed a layer of (black) silver sulfide on it either from the polluted air or the proteins from your sweaty hands—or (Heaven forbid!) you used the silver spoons for eating eggs! Wash the silverware with soap and water to remove any grease. Line a pot (stainless steel or other, but not aluminium, which will be damaged) with aluminium foil and fill the pot with enough water to cover any silverware. Add two tablespoons of baking soda and bring to boil. Then place the silverware piece by piece on the aluminium foil so that the foil touches each piece of silverware. The aluminium and silver need to make good electrical contact. Use stainless steel tongs to handle the objects in the boiling solution. When changes occur in the appearance of the silverware, remove it from the pot and wash with clean water to remove all traces of the soda. The silver is restored, literally. Unlike polishing with an abrasive, you are not removing silver, but reversing the tarnishing reaction by turning black silver sulfide back into silver metal.

(You can check the spent solution with salt water (teaspoon in a glass). If any silver had been removed and dissolved in the process it would precipitate white silver chloride. This method is also used by jewellers (particularly in Asia) to test for silver. They scrape a little of the 'silver' off. Dissolve it in nitric acid and then add salt.)

At fairs and trade exhibits, 'magic alloys' are touted which (at great expense) are claimed to do the same thing much better. These are aluminium alloys but they don't seem to offer any advantage over aluminium foil.

We discuss toxicity of aluminium on pp. 115–17.

Stainless steel

Today stainless steel pots and pans are preferred. Common stainless steel is an alloy of iron (74%), chromium (18%) and

Quantum mechanics in the kitchen

Aluminium metal, a superb electrical conductor, is always covered by a coherent layer of aluminium oxide, a superb electrical insulator. (Aluminium oxide is the basis of ceramics, and amongst the best heat and electrical insulating materials known.)

So why is it that two pieces of aluminium placed together conduct heat and electricity from one to the other through the two oxide layers?

The answer comes from quantum mechanics exerting an effect discernible on a macroscopic level. The wave function associated with the moving electron can 'tunnel' through the barrier put up by the insulator, provided the layer is not too thick.

Hmmm. Thanks but no thanks. Sorry I asked.

nickel (8%). The chromium, like aluminium, has a tough rust layer (and hence is used to cover iron in chrome plating). Nickel makes the alloy non-magnetic. Surprisingly, stainless steel is quite a poor conductor of heat and needs a copper base (sometimes covered with steel) to allow it to perform.

Stainless isn't stainless if you don't keep it spotless. Any parts left greasy will soon show rusty stains nearby. Now, it is not the grease that is the problem, it is the lack of air being able to get to the steel.

Have a look in the filing cabinet! Haul out a document held together with a (steel) paper clip that has been there for yonks. Note that the rust stains appear *under* the clip, but the rest of the clip and paper seem fine. Same story: having parts where air is absent causes rust.

Tin

Found an old letter the other day.

> Thank you very much for your interest in our canned Tomato Soup. Indeed during storage some of the tin will leach into the product. However, the practice and

Rusting bridges

Steel bridge pylons show rust at the top of the water level, but at points just below the water (with less air), the iron actually disappears, and the bridge can collapse before you see anything.

So, do you stop rusting by **allowing** air to get at the metal? You bet!

The reasons take us a bit deeper. When iron rusts, the loss of iron and the formation of rust don't occur at exactly the same place. The process is like in a torch battery with plus and minus ends to it. It is called an electrochemical reaction. If iron is uniformly exposed to air all over them this plus and minus separation does not occur. And there is no rusting.

need for tin dissolution to maintain the desired colour and flavour attribute in many fruits and vegetable products has been long established. Tinplate provides galvanic protection of the base steel by slow sacrificial dissolution of the tin coating. Using a fully lacquered can (protecting the tin from dissolving) will lead to changes in the flavour and colour which could affect consumer acceptance. The levels allowed are set for taste not toxicity reasons.

Manager, Quality Assurance, H. J. Heinz Co., Australia,
7 July 1986 [slightly edited for style].

So there you go. The tin dissolves to protect the iron, just like zinc coating protects steel in 'galvanised' iron. Hence the manager's use of the phrase 'galvanic protection'. The tin protects the contents and the container. And now that you are addicted to the tang taste, they can't leave the tin out.

One cause of a can 'blowing' is the production of hydrogen from the acid reacting with the tin. And he is right. There is no health issue. A maximum level of 250 milligrams per kilogram has been set by the food standard authorities. Most tins for other products are lacquered on the inside for added protection against food acids.

The teflon coated non-stick frypan has quite a history. There is a myth that this coating was one of the spin-offs from

The plate protection

On the outside of the can, tin gives only mechanical protection to the iron (iron is more reactive than tin in air). On the inside, in the presence of food acids (which can keep taking tin out of circulation), the reactivity is reversed.

the enormous $14 billion US effort to place a man on the moon, which came to fruition on 20 July 1969. Not so. The truth is the other way around. The frypan coating on the spaceship made possible the 'great step forward for mankind'.

Polytetrafluoroethylene was discovered in 1938 and found to have remarkable properties. DuPont called this new plastic Teflon. The trick to make it bond to aluminium was solved by a French company Tefan (tetra ethylene fluorine aluminium) in the 1950s. Its miraculous frypan dominated the market a decade before the moon landing. What did happen around lunar landing time was the discovery of another use for Teflon, namely Gore's textile or Gortex.

WATER

Why are wet T-shirts so educational?

A WET T-SHIRT party is an eye-catching demonstration of instant translucency. When water wets cotton you can suddenly see through. Why is that so?

While not so bracing, you see the same effect when a smear of butter is made on a paper towel or tissue. Cellulose fibres in paper and cotton are actually transparent. They appear opaque because individual fibres are surrounded by air, and air and fibre bend light rays very differently. They are said to have different *refractive indices* (RI).

This difference prevents light moving easily between fibres which would make the whole sheet transparent. Instead the light is reflected back to your eye from all directions and this scattering is seen as white.

Fat happens to have much the same RI as fibre, so where the fibre is surrounded by fat, light can move through the fat from one fibre to the next. Because the light is not scattered, the greasy spots on the paper become transparent. Water is not as good an RI match with fibre as fat, but the solid backing of the T-shirt wearer helps transparency!

Minimising RI differences between solids and liquids has many applications. By placing a mixed fibre fabric in a set of different liquids, the components can be made to disappear in turn, and thus identified. Gemologists and jewellers use this technique also. They can place precious stones (and their imitations) in a set of different liquids until the gem 'disappears', revealing its RI and identity.

The refractive index of glass varies depending on type,

composition and manufacturer. Thus if two pieces of glass, one from a crime scene and another from a suspect, differ in RI, it can safely be concluded that their source is different. If on the other hand their RIs are the same, then possibly they have a common origin. Forensic scientists make use of the fact that the RI of a fluid decreases slowly with increasing temperature. So they immerse the glass fragments they are comparing in an appropriate liquid on a slide under a microscope and warm the slide slowly until one fragment can no longer be seen. If both fragments disappear at the same temperature, they have the same RI, and the case goes on to other evidence. Toothpaste manufacturers match the RI of the abrasive they have included with that of the supporting liquid so that the abrasive cannot be seen. Producers of plastic mouldings make sure the RI of the cheap filler they use matches that of the expensive polymer base for the same reason.

The shimmering of the air above a hot road is due to the fluctuating refractive index of air with temperature. Different pockets of air at different temperatures bend light by slightly different angles. The shimmering can create an appearance of a water layer and this is the origin of the desert mirage.

Maximising, rather than minimising, RI differences is also very useful. Adding lead to glass increases its refractive index and makes the 'crystal' sparkle more. Diamonds have one of the highest refractive indexes.

Paint manufacturers choose their white pigment and plastic binder to have the greatest difference in RI so as to give a required whiteness with the least amount of solids. They also include small spheres filled with air because air has a quite different RI to the plastic and helps make the paint opaque, just like lots of air bubbles caught in water just released from a tap make a glass of water temporarily cloudy.

Light is kept guided inside a fibre optic cable by maximising RI differences between the optical fibre and its sheathing (or air). The same principle is applied in arty lamps with long dangling light-conducting fibre 'petals'.

The dark-light liquid level indicator on top of a dishwasher rinse fluid holder or fuel tank in a lawn mower both use the difference in RI between the liquid and air to indicate whether one or the other is in contact with a tapered plastic probe. This method is used to display the depth of fluid in a closed or sealed

Refraction in water

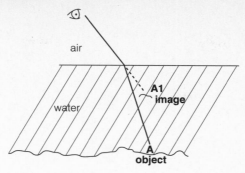

container. Similarly, the optical charge indicator in a sealed lead acid battery depends on the fact the RI of battery acid increases with charge. Here the probe stays in contact with the fluid which changes its RI. A more sophisticated version of this device is used by vintners when they measure the RI of grape juice, which is a direct indicator of sugar content, in order to make their decision on picking time.

As the song says, 'Even oysters do it'. The shells of oysters, the scales of fish and the makers of nail varnish exploit the fact that refractive index changes with the colour of light, being higher for blue and lower for red. So slight changes in angle of viewing brings out the shimmering colours of the rainbow. And this is why we have rainbows in the first place.

So throwing water over T-shirts is all done in the good cause of refractive chemistry. But why do different materials refract light differently in the first place?

If you look down into the quiet water of a pond or swimming pool the apparent bottom, A^1, is above the actual bottom, A. As the diagram above shows, the light reaching your eye from the bottom is bent at the surface, away from the vertical. The same effect occurs for an oar that is partially submerged in the water. There appears to be a sharp bend where it enters the water and the underwater part appears lifted above its actual position.

Light can be seen as obeying a so-called principle of least effort which is a bit anthropomorphic for most hard scientists. However, it is a powerful approach that is consistent with quantum mechanics and the particle-wave duality for matter and light. Light follows a route with the shortest time to travel from

Principle of least effort

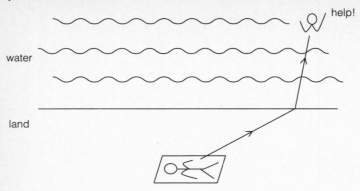

A to B. As light travels in straight lines and travels faster in air than in water, the route taken will have it spend less time in the water and more in the air. That is, it will follow a shorter path in the water and consequently a longer one in the air. The bigger the difference in speed in the two mediums, the bigger the difference in path lengths and the bigger the bend. The speed of light in different mediums can be compared by how much the light bends in going from one medium to the other, and this bending power relative to zero in a vacuum is called the refractive index (RI) of the medium. It is a ratio and you do not need to know the absolute speed of light.

Not clear? Well imagine you are sitting on a beach. Over to your right, out at sea, someone is yelling for help. You could rush off in a straight line towards the person, diving into the surf when you hit the waterline and swim out. Or you could run down the beach till you came to a spot directly opposite and swim out perpendicular so as to cover the shortest distance in the water.

The fastest path is somewhere between these two; running down most of the way on land and swimming out at an intermediate angle. Just where you enter the water depends on your relative speed in air compared with water. You will have quickly 'tried' the various paths out in your mind before setting off. Light does this too. By being a wave, all the non-optimum paths cancel each other out and disappear so only the 'best' is left. Now it's getting heavy and we'll leave it there (but see p. 192).

Dissolving into each other—when and why?

WHAT DISSOLVES WHAT and how much? It can be crucial. Sugar in the petrol, you've heard the story. Actually sugar won't dissolve in petrol, it will just sit at the bottom of the tank and, if stirred up, may clog up the fuel line.

In our bodies, combinations of certain chemicals in excess cause minerals to crystallise out of body fluids. This can cause painful stones or other conditions, depending on what you eat and how your body handles it.

Gout is caused by a uric acid salt formed from the breakdown of excess protein, while pseudo-gout is caused by precipitation of calcium pyrophosphate. The two are easily distinguished by their colours under a polarising microscope. Calcium oxalate precipitates to form kidney stones, and cholesterol is often found in gallstones.

Swallowing excessive water-soluble vitamin and mineral (e.g. vitamins B and C) supplements is less likely to be a problem than swallowing excess oil-soluble ones (like vitamins A and E) as excess water-soluble supplements are quickly secreted in the urine whereas oil-soluble ones can build up to dangerous levels in the body fat and liver.

Only a limited number of materials pass through our skin. However, these are often the ones you don't want, such as some sunscreening agents and solvents like toluene and petrol. Conversely, some desirable cosmetic nutritive agents don't get into the skin, even with lots of expensive advertising hype behind them.

Oils and acrylics

When a water-based acrylic paint is painted over an oil-based (synthetic or linseed) undercoat, you occasionally get bubbles forming which leave small round holes. This indicates 'non wetting' of the old surface by the new paint. Answer: add a few squirts of dishwashing detergent to the water-based paint and it will flow over properly. Not too much, though, otherwise you might froth up the paint.

The golden rule for stain removal is like disssolves like. Fatty stains, such as chocolate, need a solvent that will mix with oil, while 'dirt' is soluble or suspended in water. Detergent solutions give us a bit of both solvents, by being mainly water, with microscopic communes of an oil-like nature suspended inside that absorb fat and wash away.

Dry-cleaning fluids have the opposite arrangement, with micro water globules in an organic solvent. Some organic contaminants (like chewing gum) are best frozen solid (with ice) and then mechanically removed (see pp. 110 on why we wet clothes before we iron them). What you chose depends on the delicacy of the cloth as well.

Dyes used to colour cloth need to be made insoluble otherwise they'd come out in the wash (and worse, stick to something else). Lots of chemical tricks are used to achieve this, including a mordant process whereby the dye is reacted in the cloth with a metal salt, like aluminium actetate, to fix it inside the fibre.

Dinosaur bones have survived for a hundred million years because they are made from calcium phosphate which is extremely insoluble. Soft tissues and leaves survive as fossils for the same reason, but in their case it's anaerobic bacteria that produce calcium phosphate from chemicals in the invaded dead cell, often within weeks.

To release phosphate from the mineral to make superphosphate fertiliser, prolonged cooking with concentrated sulfuric acid is needed. However, the 'soluble' superphosphate so produced quickly gets bound by the soil and becomes insoluble again and so has to be replaced regularly.

Soft tissue fossils

Phosphatisation is a process that preserves soft tissue as fossils. In the substantial absence of oxygen, the tissue breaks down over several weeks into phosphates and fatty acids, and in acidic conditions, calcium phosphate forms around the decaying tissue. After decay is complete, the pH rises and calcium carbonate is deposited. This process has preserved the oldest soft tissue fossil ever found, the 520 million-year-old muscle tissue of a primitive worm ('New Scientist', 3 October 1998).

Sugar and gasoline

This letter to the editor concerning the solubility of sugar in gasoline was published in the *Journal of Forensic Science* in 1993 (vol. 38, no. 4, p. 753).

Dear Sir,

It is common folklore that sugar added to an automobile gasoline tank will cause major damage to the engine. However apocryphal this notion is, it is widely believed and has prompted at least some grudge holders to pour table sugar into the gas tanks of automobiles belonging to their enemies.

The premise that sugar added to a gasoline tank will foul an engine seems to imply that sucrose is soluble in gasoline and that the sugar will therefore be carried to the engine by the gasoline. This premise, which the present work tends to dispel, seems to be embraced by vandals and police investigators alike. Police investigators, in pursuit of 'sugared' gasoline, are more likely to submit to the laboratory samples of suspected gasoline siphoned from the tank or delivered by the fuel pump to a disconnected fuel line. Rarely will an investigator cause the entire contents of a fuel tank to be submitted to the laboratory.

Sugar can be detected in fluid gasoline only to the extent that it is soluble. Chemical principles of solubility would predict marginal if any solubility of sugar in gasoline. We demonstrate here that this is the case. From the standpoint of criminal responsibility it would make no difference whether the sugar is soluble or not, but from the standpoint of sampling and testing, it makes a great deal of difference.

Two experiments were conducted. In the first experiment, a carefully weighed amount of oven dried sucrose was added to gasoline at room temperature and stirred for 30 minutes. The mixture was filtered through tared filter paper; the filter paper containing undissolved sucrose was oven dried, allowed to cool, and weighed. The recovery of sucrose in replicate runs was, respectively, 97.97% and 99.58%. While this experiment suggests that sucrose is virtually insoluble in gasoline, the limits of sensitivity of the method do not put the issue at rest.

A second experiment was conducted in which a known amount of 14C labeled sucrose was added to a known amount of gasoline. The mixture was equilibrated by stirring and an aliquot taken for scintillation counting. The detected concentration of 14C labeled sucrose in gasoline ranged in replicate experiments between 1.26 mg/L and 1.44 mg/L. If the upper limit is rounded off to 1.5 mg/L, then the total amount of sucrose that would go into solution in a 15 gallon tank of gas would be on the order of 90 mg.

The implications of the solubility of sucrose in gasoline to sampling and analytical considerations are patent. If sugar is added to gasoline, virtually all of it will be found, undissolved, on the bottom of the tank. Even if the gasoline is saturated with sucrose, the concentration of sucrose is too low to be detected by simple means. A 100 mL sample of gasoline, for example, would contain only 150%ug of sucrose. Accordingly, the investigation of cases of motor fouling caused by the suspected addition of sugar to the gasoline must include a sampling of any solid residues in the fuel tank.

Keith Inman, M. Crim.
George F. Sensabaugh, D. Crim., Senior Criminalist
John I. Thornton, D. Crim.,
California Dept of Justice DNA Laboratory

Glenn Hardin, M. P. H. Criminalist
Minnesota Bureau of Criminal Apprehension

What's really *in* the water?

H_2O IS THE chemical formula for water and that is pretty well general knowledge. Less well known is that by rights it shouldn't be a liquid. After all, its next of kin H_2S 'rotten egg gas' and H_3N and H_4C (ammonia and methane—formulas reordered to show the relationship) are all gases at room temperatures.

In a water molecule the hydrogen-oxygen-hydrogen is bent at an angle of about 110 degrees. This means that touchy-feely oxygen components of one water molecule can bond fleetingly with the hydrogens on another. These flirtations hold all water molecules together strongly enough to keep water as a liquid.

The resulting promiscuous structure in which they are all bonding is so open that when water freezes, the solid is light enough to float on the liquid (water has its maximum density at +4°C). It is highly unusual for any liquid to be denser than the solid it freeezes to. In fact it is difficult to think of any other material that has this amazing property.

In rivers, water freezes from the top down rather than bottom up. Just as well, otherwise fish would be separated from their worms, and the worms from their air. Aquatic life as we know it would not exist.

Water is a very good solvent and dissolves surprising amounts of everything. There is about 6 millilitres of oxygen in every litre of water, so fish can have lungs on their skin (gills).

As temperature rises, air bubbles out. Gases become less soluble in water with increasing temperature. Fish kills are often due to lack of oxygen in the water from a temperature rise rather

Typefreeze

Type metal is a lead alloy with antimony and traces of other metals. When the hot metal was poured into the mould in the days of pre-computer typesetting it expanded slightly on freezing and so filled the finest detail of the mould. On further cooling it contracted again and was thus easily removed from the mould.

than from more sinister causes. Some fish in the Bering Strait near Alaska lack haemoglobin because there is enough oxygen dissolved in the cold water to make additional storage in blood unnecessary.

Demineralised or distilled water is tasteless, and if drunk in huge quantities, can strip your body of essential minerals and eventually put you in a coma. The dissolved salts are what makes water taste. Bottled waters use sources with good mineral content or 'adjust' them appropriately. If you read the label it nearly always states that the *typical* contents are as listed, that is, they are hardly ever measured and checked.

Micro creepy crawlies find water a great home as well as dissolved minerals. Many of these do terrible things to our gut. There are two general approaches to eviction. One is to burn the little buggers out. Now, visiting fire persons will tell you that water is not going to burst into flame if you blow air onto it, so burning in the traditional sense is out. But one of oxygen's relatives, chlorine, *will* 'burn' in water, and (in the form of pool chlorine or bleach) does a pretty good job on most microbes and bodily wastes.

Bushwalkers in recent years have been faced with giardia which needs treatment from chlorine's big brother, iodine. In swimming pools with cryptosporidium, oxygen's big brother, ozone, can be effective.

The alternative to burning is burying alive. It has been traditional to clarify muddy water by using aluminium salts. The clay particles tend to be negatively charged and aluminium salts form a triply positively charged ion. On collision the two stick together and neutralise each other's electrical charge. The particles then floculate (forms flocks) and the bigger lumps fall to the bottom. The same principle applies to the use of

Liquid gas

Most solids dissolve better as you heat the solvent (e.g. sugar in water), but for gases it is invariably the other way. Warming a Coke makes it go flat. Why?

Dissolving a gas in a liquid is a bit like having to first liquify the gas then mixing the two liquids together. The higher the temperature the harder it is to liquify a gas. This results in less gas dissolving at higher temperatures.

aluminium salts in antiperspirants and sticks for stopping bleeding from shaving nicks.

Many microbes (including the two above) are also negatively charged and will be pulled down with the clay. Sydney Water apparently dropped the use of aluminium, allegedly because of possible links with Alzheimer's disease, and used iron (steel works' waste) instead. However, iron is not as good a precipitant as aluminium, as Sydneysiders learnt.

Fluoride in the water,
a good idea?

I REMEMBER HOW annoyed I was when I arrived in Canberra at the end of 1964 to discover that the Federal Government had decided by fiat to fluoridate Canberra's water supply without consultation with the populace.

The columns of the *Canberra Times* were filled with letters complaining about all sorts of ills. Cats had lost their fur, bathtubs were turning green (true, but this was due to excessive chlorine levels and hot weather combining to leach copper from the plumbing), teeth were discolouring overnight and so on. A week or so after the torrent had subsided, there was a small announcement in the paper that because of technical problems in the distribution mechanism, fluoridation had been delayed. It was generally accepted that bureaucrats lacked the sense of humour to have deliberately planned this ploy.

Back in 1931 the Aluminium Company of America (ALCOA) analysed the water supply of the town in which its factory was situated. It was concerned that the fluoride that it used in its smelting operations in the town of Bauxite was entering the drinking water and causing mottled teeth. It was right. Levels were between 2 and 13 parts per million and matched those found in areas of high natural fluoride content in water, such as in Colorado.

Only when a complete survey was done on natural fluoride levels and mottled teeth throughout the United States was the further correlation with tooth decay discovered. The trick then was to find an optimum compromise level.

Continuous applications of low levels of fluoride reduce

dental caries. There are a number of chemical mechanisms that suggest why this should be the case. There is also considerable epidemiological evidence used to support the efficacy of fluoridation. However, a study in Canberra itself showed that a reduction in tooth decay continued well after the ten years beyond which the effect of fluoride would have been expected to level out.

Such data as there were seemed to show that the more fluoride in the water supply the more the decay was reduced until you reach 1 part per million. On a graph the amount of improvement above this level flattened out, and was not worth the increased risk of other problems. Fluoridation is generally achieved by adding solid sodium silicofluoride so as to provide 1 milligram of fluoride to one litre of water, with an error margin of 10 per cent. The level determined was based on the assumption that this was the only significant source of the element. Dosing water at 1 part per million, means ingesting 1 milligram of fluoride for every litre of water drunk. Such low levels of fluoride in the water supply are harmless beyond reasonable doubt for all but a minority. Amongst this minority are people who drink really excessive amounts of water, diabetics, patients undergoing dialysis and people with defective kidneys. Arguments about fluoride causing cancer have been discounted, although there are problems with bone diseases at much higher levels of fluoridation.

Is the decision taken for Canberra in 1964 still appropriate today? What has changed in the last 33 years?

Because our methods of analysis have improved enormously, we are better aware of the background fluoride level in our water supply (0.2 to 0.3 ppm) and other dietary sources of fluoride. Processing food and beverages with fluoridated water makes a contribution to our daily intake commensurate with that coming from fluoridated water alone. Other sources of fluoride are spinach, gelatine, bone meal and fish protein. Tea provides approximately 0.12 milligrams per cup above the level in the water.

We are all more affluent, middle class and better exposed to public health messages. Products have changed as well. It takes effort to buy a toothpaste today which does not contain fluoride in one form or another. The levels in toothpaste are of the order of 1000 parts per million. Children under five are the highest swallowers of toothpaste and absorb about 0.3 milligrams of fluoride per brushing.

Non-fluoridated cities, such as Brisbane, have no higher level of dental caries than otherwise similar fluoridated cities. It is very likely that fluoride from these other sources (including soft drinks imported into Brisbane from fluoridated areas) is the reason, although this is still disputed. There is thus a very good case for keeping the water used for (most) soft drinks fluoridated at the current level.

Can you make a personal decision to remove fluoride from your own water supply? Remember we are talking about a level of a material in water of 1 part per million parts of water. We are also not talking about a controlled laboratory experiment with very small water samples, but kilolitres of water passing through unattended and unserviced home filtering units. For all practical purposes, once the fluoride is in, there is no economical way of removing it. Otherwise those towns that have excessive natural fluoride in their water supplies would have reduced it to 1 part per million.

What can you learn
by osmosis?

I WAS ENGROSSED in a *Choice* magazine. The lead article was 'Water Purifiers: do they work?'.

'Would you like sugar in your tea?' asked my spouse. The article was so interesting I wasn't listening carefully. 'Thanks,' I said. 'Woops. I'm sorry, I really meant no thanks!'

Tough luck, too late. That's chemistry.

Adding sugar to tea and stirring is easy. Removing the added sugar afterwards is impossible without a lot of ingenuity and effort. This simple example illustrates a fundamental fact of nature. Processes which appear to go easily on their own in one direction are difficult to reverse. In scientific terms this is known as the principle of increasing entropy. Things mix naturally but don't unmix.

In a wider sense we continuously want to 'take the sugar out of tea'. Purifying water is a major health requirement across the world. Waste-water treatment, desalination, even removing fluoride and chlorine from water in private dwellings are areas of increasing demand. In each case you want to keep the bath water and throw away the baby—some of the materials that are dissolved in the water.

For some applications the idea is reversed. The aim is to keep the dissolved material and throw away the water! Making orange juice concentrate from fresh juice is a good example. With alcoholic drinks you might want to go either way. You might want to take the alcohol out of wine to produce a non- or low-alcohol beverage, or you might want to take some of the water out to make spirits.

Mixing a glass of sugar syrup with a glass of water dilutes the syrup and concentrates the water. If you consider a glass of syrup in the form of a red blood cell and place it in water and view it under a microscope, what do you see? The walls of the cell are semi-permeable. This means the cell walls will let water through, but will not let the soluble contents of the cell out. As the 'syrup' can't move out of the cell, the water moves in. This is the only way mixing of water and 'syrup' can now occur. However, this means the cell will swell. The elastic walls stretch as the water enters and the elastic stretch acts against further water entering.

It is to prevent swelling of bodily cells that medical fluids, ranging from intravenous drips to simple solutions for bathing wounds, are made up with dissolved materials at a concentration equal to that found in body cells. On the other hand, if the medical fluid is more concentrated than in the cell, water moves from the cell out into the fluid and the cell shrivels. The bathing solution doesn't have to have the same materials dissolved in it, as long as their effective concentration has the same 'mixing pressure'. In the trade this is called *isotonic*. The word 'isotonic' has nothing to do with tonics. The term is related to muscle tone.

The pressure of the water trying to enter a concentrated solution is enormous. It is called osmotic pressure, from the Greek *osmos*, to push. It can amount in height to the equivalent of tens of metres of water pressure. To reverse the flow requires pressures of this magnitude in the opposite direction. Water purifiers using so called reverse osmosis are based on this principle of exerting pressure in the opposite direction.

In our bodies, the kidneys work as a reverse osmosis water purification system. The kidneys conserve and purify water by concentrating waste products behind membranes, and excreting them to the bladder. Making dilute solutions more concentrated, is a form of unmixing. The pressure needed for this reverse osmosis comes from the blood pressure. If thickening of the arteries causes too great a loss of pressure, then the process slows and stops. High blood pressure is the body's attempt to overcome the loss due to clogged pipes, but eventually this may fail and we become bloated from fluid retention and poisoned by our own waste products.

In a dialysis unit, technology mimics the kidney. Supplying

pressure is easy. Developing the correct membrane that will distinguish between substances that need to be held from those that need to pass through is difficult.

Controlling the dynamic movement of water and being able to select those substances which will move backwards and forwards across a membrane has significant commercial significance far beyond just dialysis machines.

What drives these movements of water? The tendency to mix is the simple answer. The 'chemical potential' is the jargon used by chemists, because the drive can be measured in terms of the potential energy of a head of water needed to oppose the movement. It is amazing that this desire to mix can generate such huge pressures.

This drive accounts for the movement of water into the cells of the roots of trees. The water then moves up the trunk, helped on its way by evaporation from the leaves at the top, which provides an additional 'upward drag'. So there is a lot you can learn by osmosis!

There are many other examples of such processes. When you make jam, you add a great deal of sugar. The reason for this is only partially to help it set. The main reason is to preserve the product. Because of its high sugar content, any cells of microbes that drift into the jam will be shrunk by having their water dragged out. The contents of their cells then become too concentrated for the organism to continue to operate. However, mould can begin to grow under the lid where water may have evaporated out of the hot jam after pouring into the jar and condensed again under the lid, leaving the sugar behind. The protection of a concentrated sugar solution is gone and the mould thrives. Salting food serves the same purpose. Sugar or salt, it doesn't matter, as long as the dissolved substances are concentrated enough to dehydrate microbes.

Why superslurpers slurp

WE DON'T THINK of plastics dissolving in water, but some are designed to do just that. Pick the common factor in the following:

1. Toxic shock can be caused by highly absorbent tampons.
2. When some potting mixes are left outside in the rain, little lumps of jelly appear.
3. Plastic crocodiles grow bigger in fresh water than in salt water.

These effects are all achieved courtesy of a material called 'superslurper', generally made by linking together two polymers. One is acrylic and the other often a modified starch.

This so-called hydrolysed-starch polyacrylonitrile copolymer comes in many forms depending on how long the pieces of each partner are, the relative amount of each partner and the number of cross-links between chains.

The product gets its nickname because it slurps up lots of water, swells up, and finally turns into a jelly. It can take up to 2000 times its weight in water. You can also dry it out again and reuse it. Its swelling capacity decreases the more you cross-link but this then makes the product more elastic.

Why does it suck up and swell? The cause is electric! When the plastic sucks in water, it throws off positive hydrogen ions into the water leaving negative charges behind in the plastic. Like charges repel. This repulsion forces the polymer chains apart. Water then penetrates further and the polymer keeps on expanding as fast as the water can enter. The cross-links stop it dissolving all together. (See later, PVA, where they do dissolve completely.)

Really important is that the nature of the polymer prevents the water being squeezed out again. In baby nappies and in incontinence pads the material absorbs up to 30 times its weight in urine and retains it under pressure (gravity or squeezing). This has led to thinner, more comfortable nappies and drier babies. In tampons, the efficiency is compromised by the increased risk of bacterial growth and the possibility of toxic shock syndrome.

Some small toy crocodiles and other plastic toys are made with superslurper. When placed in water these toys swell up. The ultimate size of the crocodile depends on the purity of the water. Salts present in the water reduce the swelling because they weaken the force with which the negative charges on the jelly chains repel one another. The more salt the less swelling.

Because of the danger of these toys being swallowed and then swelling in the stomach, they are banned in Australia. A related polymer, however, is sold as an appetite suppressant because it also swells up inside the stomach and makes the person feel full.

Superslurpers have uses in gardening and agriculture for increasing the water holding capacity of sandy soils and potting mixtures. Roots thrive in the material. However, high soil salt content, particularly calcium, reduces the effectiveness markedly.

Another use for superslurpers is as moulds for metal castings. A level of only one per cent is sufficient to bind sand firmly enough for this purpose. A couple of enterprising PhD graduates in Germany developed this product from test tube into a major international company Stockhausen. This is the sort of fast swelling we all dream about.

Another water-friendly plastic, polyvinylalcohol (PVA), can be used to form the white water-soluble latex in wood glue or engineered chemically for use as a permanent plastic film, or designed for something in between these two extremes. For example there are some things in life that you just don't want to get your hands on. These include bags of infectious hospital laundry and bags of prepackaged toxic concentrates of chemicals for agricultural sprays. In both cases, the sealed bags can be thrown into water (the laundry tub or the spray tank), and the

Making PVA slime

Once water has pushed the polymer chains apart, we can now link them up again in a very special way and produce a very strange product.

Recipe 1
Measure 25 mL white (wood) glue into a cup
Stir in 20 mL water
Add food colouring if desired
Stir in 5 mL borax solution
Place cup on paper towel and remove stirrer
Store in plastic bag until needed

Recipe 2
Add a 20x20 cm piece of PVA bag to 25 mL water
Stir well to dissolve (hot water for laundry bags)
Add food colouring
Add 5 mL borax solution
Store in plastic bag until needed

When pulled slowly, the slime mixture flows. It will even self-siphon out of its container, but try cutting the stream with a pair of scissors and it stiffens it up and it becomes elastic. In fact slime will bounce a little. It behaves in exactly the opposite way to materials like quicksand or water-based latex paints, which become more fluid when stressed.

A great toy for kids, but it goes mouldy in a few days and should be thrown into the garbage in a plastic bag.

bag dissolves to safely release its contents, untouched by human hands. These PVA bags come as warm-water soluble (WWS) or cold-water soluble (CWS) types. In contrast to the super-slurper, this polymer dissolves completely in water.

This has revolutionised safety in both these industries. The bags are probably too expensive for general use, say, for shopping, but they would be environmentally more benign than what we presently use. You will be more familiar with soluble PVA as the active component in white (wood) glue. The water initially holds the pieces of wood together (but a clamp helps).

As the object dries out, the PVA changes into a form that is no longer soluble in water forming a strong link to the wood. The strength of the bond depends on the area not the thickness, so only a thin layer of glue should be used.

Why damp clothes
iron better

ALL PLASTICS SHARE a common structure. A good analogy is a bowl of cooked spaghetti where the strands represent the molecules of a polymer or plastic material. They are all tangled together. At low temperatures the mass sets and plastics appear solid and brittle, like ordinary glass. On warming, the long spaghetti-like molecules in the plastic start to wriggle, and slip by each other and eventually move and flow cooperatively, giving a slow change with temperature from solid to liquid unlike the sharp melting of non-plastic materials.

This so-called glass transition temperature (Tg), marks a temperature of increase in flowability, rather than a sharp melting point. Tg varies between different plastics and is lowered by adding plasticisers. Solid PVC is heavily plasticised to make it rubbery.

We tend to forget that the original and still very useful plastics were natural. Natural chewing gum is based on gutta-percha, a perverse form of natural rubber. It's hard to remove gum from carpet because it is gooey and sticks. But if you first freeze it with iceblocks to bring it below its Tg, it will break off cleanly like a solid. Most chewing gum today is made from synthetic PVA (polyvinyl acetate). It behaves in a similar fashion.

Cotton is a natural polymer of cellulose with a Tg of 225°C, so the fabrics made from its fibres tend to keep their shape. Water added to cotton acts as a plasticiser and lowers the Tg, making it 'plastic', and so allowing wrinkles to be removed easily. Hot ironing removes the water and on cooling the new shape is 'frozen' in.

Cotton slowly absorbs water from the air and reverts to being more plastic and easily wrinkled again. Blends with polyester tend to be less absorbent. When a hot clothes dryer is used for cotton towels and nappies, water is removed while the fabric is hot and above its Tg. The tumbling prevents the material setting in a cramped state and tumbling must be kept up during the cooling phase. But on the washing line with temperatures below the Tg, the evaporating water just leaves the item to dry and set in its matted state.

Nylon and polyester have a lower Tg and so a cooler iron needs to be used. Steam is used to iron wool, but here the reason is to break the disulfide bonds of the wool protein that keep wool fibres in shape. They re-form in the new shape on cooling. Hair is also temporarily reset with water (see p. 138). Silk, like wool, is also a protein fibre (Tg 162^0C), but because of its smooth filaments, water has difficulty penetrating it. Putting moist silk into the freezer for half an hour appears to help ironing. Perhaps cooling gives more time for the plasticising water to spread through the fabric without evaporating.

Perhaps. As irons aren't made from iron any more, I must go back to some more 'aluminiuming'.

METALS

Aluminium and Alzheimer's disease—a connection?

WHILE ALUMINIUM SALTS are toxic to nerves, they have difficulty passing through the gut lining. In the acidic stomach, ingested aluminium is there in the ionic form Al^{3+}, and ions can't pass through the lining. In the alkaline small intestine it is there in the form of insoluble hydroxide, which physically cannot pass through. There are some complexes of aluminium, notably citrate (formed with citric acid in fruit juices, for example) which are neutral and can pass through the gut. Water is a minor source of aluminium in the diet and unlikely to contribute significantly to bodily absorption. Absorbed aluminium is stored mainly in the bones.

There is no doubt that aluminium is neurotoxic. Renal dialysis patients exposed to aluminium in the dialysis fluid, for example, will suffer dementia (but not Alzheimer's).

There is evidence of short-term toxicity with excess aluminium. In Britain, a population of about 20 000 individuals was exposed for at least five days to increased levels of aluminium sulfate, accidentally placed in a drinking water facility. Reports of nausea, vomiting, diarrhoea, mouth ulcers, skin ulcers, skin rashes and arthritic pain were noted. No lasting effects on health could be attributed to the known exposures from aluminium in the drinking water. It was concluded that the symptoms of this massive overexposure were mild and short lived.

Adults consume between 2.5 and 13 milligrams daily of aluminium from food and beverages. Drinking water is generally clarified using alum as a flocculating agent. This precipitates out suspended clay (a source of insoluble aluminium) and leaves

Further chemical details

Aluminium occurs in two main types in water. In mildly acidic solutions (pH<5.5), it occurs as the aluminium ion attached to six water molecules $(Al^{3+}(H_2O)_6)$. At pH>7, aluminium is present as aluminates $Al(OH)_3$ of varying degrees of insolubility depending on what else is around that can complex the aluminium (K_{sp} for gibbsite—the pure hydroxide—is about 10^{-9}). The highest concentration for aluminium occurs at near neutral pH and is about 3×10^{-11} moles per litre or 0.8 micrograms per litre. Fluoride forms strong complexes with aluminium and at concentrations of 10^{-4} to 10^{-5} moles per litre, the complexes AlF_2+ and AlF_3o are the most common kinds.

behind extra soluble aluminium which contributes about 0.2 milligrams per day (up to 0.4 mg/day) in the drinking water. In comparison, absorption in the lungs for non-occupationally exposed people is up to 0.04 milligrams per day (IPCS Environmental Health Criteria for Aluminium Task Force Conclusions, UNEP, WHO, ILO, 28 April 1995). However, two average-sized antacid tablets may contain in excess of 500 milligrams of aluminium.

Some aluminium compounds are used in processed foods. Aluminium phosphate and aluminium silicate (both acid-soluble) are used for pH stabilisation, emulsifying, thickening, rising and anticaking. (In bread the range can be from 0.35 milligrams/kg up to 13 milligrams/kg in pumpernickel.)

Most antiperspirants contain aluminium chlorhydrate, which appears not to be absorbed into the bloodstream. (See also p. 139.)

While the aluminium ion cannot cross the wall of the acidic stomach, and the insoluble hydroxide cannot cross the wall of the alkaline duodenum, neutral soluble complexes of aluminium with carboxylic acids, particularly some with citrate in acid solution, are transportable across the gut wall. Citrate is a normal dietary breakdown product in the gut, as well as a common food (beverage) component. The aluminium content of citric beverages in aluminium cans has been reported to rise at up to 0.9 milligrams per litre per year of storage.

Particularly if scoured with steel wool or gritty powder,

some aluminium pans corrode more easily than others and release more aluminium into cooked foods and boiled water. Acidic foods attack the protective oxide layer. Wine and egg-yolk sauces are known to discolour in aluminium pans.

There is little correlation between total aluminium ingested and the amount taken up into the bloodstream (i.e. bioavailability) because of the way aluminium is complexed. For example, tea has high aluminium levels (1000 to 3000 micrograms/L) but very little is absorbed because the aluminium occurs as complexes with polyphenols which are poorly digested. Aluminium is taken up from water with decreasing efficiency in the presence of lemon juice > orange juice > wine, coffee > tomato juice > beer > tea and milk. The presence of citrate can raise blood plasma levels of aluminium independent of the level of aluminium intake.

Most Melbourne water is not treated with alum, while most Brisbane water is treated. The levels for Melbourne water are below 0.05 milligrams per litre soluble (<0.1 mg/L total), while Brisbane regions are below 0.10 milligrams per litre soluble (0.2 mg/L total). There is thus not much difference between treated and untreated water. The United States Environmental Protection Agency sets a maximum limit for aluminium in drinking water ranging from 0.05 to 0.2 milligrams per litre (depending on water source), designed to prevent precipitation of aluminium salts in the distribution system—that is, related entirely to aesthetics. Water filters remove particulates and so reduce aluminium in raw water but not treated water. The aluminium speciation at the reservoir may not correlate well with that at the household tap because of precipitation, com-plexation or release along the reticulation path.

Aluminium readily substitutes for calcium in the bones, and bone acts as a passive reservoir so that the aluminium level in the bones is a good measure of long-term exposure. It ranges from a normal 3.3 micrograms per gram of dry mass to in excess of 200 micrograms per gram of dry mass for persons on a high aluminium diet.

It seems unlikely that aluminium is a cause of Alzheimer's disease but its presence in the brain is an indicator for the disease.

How magnesium metal can sharpen your mind and a pencil

YOU MIGHT THINK the pencil sharpener is really a secret ploy to help resource-strapped science teachers. Buy a metallic pencil sharpener for a dollar and sharpen your mind.

Close inspection shows it to be a sophisticated corrosion cell. Its rectangular body is made of 92.7 per cent magnesium (others are made from aluminium or zinc), to which is attached a short steel anode with a sharp edge to increase the charge density (like in a lightning conductor).

Add a few centimetres' depth of water to an empty PET soft drink bottle then add a teaspoon of salt. Shake to dissolve. Now drop in the said object and observe. Large numbers of gas bubbles quickly form on the blade (only) and rise to the surface. The object becomes covered in a transient black film which quickly converts to lumps of fluffy white flocculant. Chloride ions from the salt destroy magnesium's protective oxide layer and allow the reaction to proceed.

The gas released is the very flammable hydrogen. You could stopper the bottle and work out how much pressure will build up from the weight of the pencil sharpener body and the volume of the bottle. Perhaps you'd like to fill a balloon. (Helium is safer for balloons and in spite of being twice as heavy as hydrogen, volume for volume, has 92 per cent of the lift. Why? Ask Archimedes.)

The white gel is magnesium hydroxide—a common antacid for upset stomachs for those who don't want to take in aluminium. Steel is the ideal anode for the reduction of water to hydroxide and is used industrially in producing caustic soda by electrolysis.

A sintered porous pad made from a composite of a powdered alloy of magnesium and iron (with polythene) was developed by the US army as a heat source for a Meal Ready to Eat (MRE) during the Desert Storm operation in Iraq. The pad is packed around an aluminium food pack, 30 millilitres of water added, and salt released from the pad starts the reaction which heats the food to about 60°C in twelve to fifteen minutes.

In Western Australia it was tradition to use the saltwater corrosion of magnesium alloy strips as a time fuse holding down the buoys that indicate the position of lobster pots below the ocean surface. The strips kept the position of the pots secret from potential poachers (and inspectors). The time to surface was controlled by the thickness of the strip.

Now what else interesting can I find in the supermarket for a dollar (plus GST)?

Chrome sweet chrome

CHROMIUM ON NICKEL plating is used to protect the underlying steel from rust and provide an attractive surface.
Chrome plating practices had to be revisited several agonising
times because simple chemical logic failed.

From the theory of (electro)chemistry, the susceptibility
(redox potentials) of metals to attack by oxygen in the air
(oxidising/rusting) is expected to worsen as you move from iron
to nickel and from nickel to chromium. In real life this is found
to be precisely wrong.

You have to protect iron and you do this by plating first
the nickel and then on top of that the chromium. Chromium
(like aluminium) doesn't rust. It quickly oxidises and forms a
coherent oxide layer that protects it from further attack. But
chromium plate always has defects (holes) in it and this allows
the metal underneath to be attacked. Nickel is interposed. By
sacrificing itself to corrosion, it saves the iron even if it doesn't
cover it everywhere. Nickel's 'rust' is white, washes off and is
not noticed much. But as the sacrifice becomes too great, it
leaves big areas of iron exposed. Iron rust breaks through.

The early 1960s saw the chromium-plated accessories on
many cars become stained with rust after only a few years. So,
next layer of logic? Make the chromium layer thicker so as to
have fewer holes. This solution made matters considerably
worse. Why? Really deep logic.

There is a (cathodic) reaction taking place on the chromium
surface (which just acts as a host and is unaffected) between
oxygen from the air and acid (hydrogen ions) in the water on

the accessory. They do this by ripping off an electron from the underlying nickel. This process alone determines the rate at which the nickel dissolves.

So a thicker layer of chromium means fewer holes through to the nickel, and in turn means fewer spots where the nickel is forced to dissolve. As the amount that must dissolve stays the same, more has to dissolve at those fewer remaining holes. Result? Bigger nickel bare spots (and consequent rust stains) occur much faster.

Thus the really deep answer was to have a thinner (not thicker) layer of chromium! Then there would be lots and lots of defects. This would mean the attack on the nickel layer was spread around. The amount of attack didn't change, it was fixed by that cathodic process, but less attack on the nickel occurred at any one particular spot. Result? Longer lasting, glittering chromium for the cars of the seventies.

It is much the same story with stainless-steel cutlery. Stainless steel is an alloy, not a plating, of iron, nickel and chromium. The common mark 18:8 stainless means 18% chromium to 8% nickel with 74% iron.

You want to prove that stainless isn't and get rust stains on your cutlery? Not a problem. As was saw on pages 82–3, just leave little dabs of muck on the surface and soon you'll have rust stains nearby (in the grain boundaries of the alloy). Exactly the same chemistry with yet another super-logical twist. To keep stainless stainless make sure all of it is exposed to lots of oxygen in the air.

The same is true of stainless-steel tow-bar balls. When covered with a tight hood to keep out the elements, the ball will rust profusely under the protection.

Why some metals
are foiled

THERE IS NO more boring way of starting a chemistry course than with a theoretical discussion of the electronic structure of atoms, orbitals, valency and so on. Agree?

Why not start in a supermarket and buy a roll of aluminium foil. Then go to the hardware store and buy some lead and copper foil. We might even splurge at the jeweller's and get gold and silver foil. But that is about it. We cannot buy zinc foil even though zinc is cheaper than copper! You can get nickel, chromium and iron as wire, but never their close neighbour cobalt.

Playing with pieces of different metals shows that the really striking difference is in the way they behave physically, when we hammer them or stretch them or twist them. Why?

The answer can be obtained via a heap of about 50 ping-pong balls, polystyrene balls, marbles, etc. Group some together tightly in one layer, like at the start of a snooker game. Place another layer on top of the first, in the indentations created by the first layer. The two layers are of course not directly on top of one another. Then place a third layer on top of the second. *Wait*! There are *two* ways you can do this. They can be placed so that the third layer is *directly* over the first layer or they can be placed such that *all three layers are all in different positions*. In the first case you can continue to pack layers alternately, while in the second case you repeat the pattern every three layers.

We can call these different packing arrangements **ab** and **abc**. The packing efficiency for the **ab** and **abc** arrangements is the same—they are the most efficient possible. In both cases each sphere is surrounded by twelve nearest neighbours. For equal-sized spheres, geometry shows that in both cases the spheres occupy 74 per cent of the total volume. If your geometry is not up to proving this, you can 'use your marbles' and pack them into an empty ice-cream tub (or other large container). Fill it with water to a level near the top of the marbles then pour the water out into another container, measure its volume, and compare it to the volume of the empty tub at the same height. (You will have an error due to 'edge effects' at the bottom, sides and top, which will be small if the marbles are small compared with the size of the container.)

The balls or marbles we have been playing with represent atoms. The best way to obtain a feel for the structures of different metals is to prepare triangular planes of these balls (atoms) just as in snooker and stick them together (polystyrene balls can be stuck with dichloromethane solvent [methylene chloride paint stripper]). Make the triangles of decreasing size, then place one triangular layer on top of another. If you pile up the layers in an **abc** arrangement then you will form a pyramid on the triangular base. In fact it is a tetrahedron where the three other faces have the atoms in layers just like the base layer. There are thus four directions in which the balls are layered. On the other hand, if you pile the layers up **ab**, the layers will alternate in jutting out and in as you go up. If you look down from the top to the base you will see channels going through the whole structure in position **c** which has been kept clear. There will be no new planes of atoms formed, only the horizontal ones you have been working on.

Metals (or alloys) that are packed **abc** are much easier to shape than those that are packed **ab**, because it is the planes of atoms that move and make metals *ductile* and *malleable*. Only metals that pack as **abc** are found in foils and wire.

This simple story does not give all the answers but it makes the concept of atoms as spheres very useful.

Tin is the Oscar Wilde of metals. It is a little uncertain as to its status as a 'real' metal and shows some outrageous behaviour. Because tin is available as a foil you would predict that it packs **abc**, and it does, almost. Tin is soft and weak; it melts at 232°C. Lead added to tin lowers this even further and gives us pewter, although for health reasons modern 'pewter' tends to tin with no lead but with just a little copper to keep it safe.

On the other hand, a small amount of tin added to copper strengthens it enormously and this piece of technology, which science now makes understandable, gave us the Bronze Age, which lasted two millenniums and allowed the development of civilisation as we know it.

A piece of pure tin when bent backwards and forwards near your ear can be heard to produce a plaintive 'cry'. This is due to presence of 'twinned' crystals in the metal which you are cruelly separating. Tin suffers from a thermodynamic 'disease'. Below 13°C the atoms of tin very slowly change their packing arrangements. In practice you need a much lower temperature to see this happen in a reasonable time. The new structure is *not a metal structure* at all (tin is as closely related to the non-metal semiconductors such as germanium as it is to the metals), and in this form it is grey and crumbly. For this reason pure tin is not much used today but historically tin 'pest' had its consequences. Men of Napoleon's army lost their trousers in the freezing winter of 1812 when their tin buttons crumbled away. Another cold Russian winter in 1867 to 1868 was said to be responsible for the rumour that the Russian hoard of silver had turned to powder. It was actually tin.

We see tin mainly in tin-plated cans. These are generally lacquered internally, but if not, a little tin dissolves in the natural vegetable acids and gives the contents its special colour and flavour. This is deliberately done for tomato soup. (See pages 83–5 for more on tin in the kitchen.)

COSMETICS

Lipsticks, but don't swallow

I N 1770 A bill was allegedly introduced into the British Parliament that read:

> . . . that all women, of whatever age, rank, profession or degree, whether virgins, maids, or widows, that shall . . . impose upon, seduce and betray into matrimony, any of His Majesty's subjects by the scents, paints, cosmetic washes, artificial teeth, false hair, Spanish wool, iron stays, hoops, high heeled shoes, bolstered hips, shall incur the penalty of the law in force against witchcraft and like misdemeanors and that the marriage, upon conviction, shall stand null and void.

Lipsticks can alter your appearance, widening narrow lips, narrowing broad lips. A greasy base makes the lips alluringly moist.

Your lipstick is a tube filled with an oil-wax base containing anti-oxidant, preservative, perfume and colour. It has to be intensely coloured to provide *good coverage*; uniform, shiny but not too greasy; it has to keep its form and consistency in reasonable temperatures; be usable in cold temperatures without crumbling or breaking; be stable to light, moisture and air; non-toxic and non-irritant; and neutral in taste.

As well as all this, lipsticks should be safe. Some of the early lipstick pigments were suspected of causing stomach cancer. In males! Either the pigments or the kissing techniques have improved. The lips need to withstand a fair bit of mechanical stress and the pigments used have to be robust. This has led to the use of pigment lakes of the type common in dyeing fabric. These are combinations of dyes with metals such as aluminium, barium, calcium and strontium. Various combinations are banned in various jurisdictions.

A lipstick should pass the 'droop point' test. This is the temperature at which lipstick lying flat in its case will droop against the case and ooze oil or flatten out. The droop point should be over 45°C and preferably over 50°C.

The colours used must be insoluble in water, otherwise you would lick them off in no time. Thus the dyes used are generally oil-soluble. They include brilliant blue, erythrosine, amaranth, rhodamine, tartrazine and eosin (tetrabromofluorescein, coded by the USA as D&C Red No. 21). Eosin is orange at low pH but when applied to the more alkaline lips it produces a relatively indelible purple stain. Unfortunately eosin and some of its relatives can cause sensitisation and allergy, often induced by sunlight.

Modern lipsticks were introduced after World War I. They were coloured with carmine, a dye and acid-base indicator made from cochineal, a small red insect, by powdering the dried insect and extracting the colour with ammonia. The cochineal insect breeds on several species of cacti (*Opuntia*) in tropical Central America (Mexico). The female of the species (*Coccus cacti*) is the source of carmine.

Indelible lipsticks were introduced in the 1920s. The dyes in these lipsticks had little colour in the tube but became coloured on reacting with the lips and stayed on for many hours. Tussy and Tangee natural lipsticks were introduced in 1925 and remained popular until the 1950s. In the 1960s the pale, lipless look was popular and there was no need for long-lasting qualities. Today, however, we are back to the twenties, but with the additional twist of colour-changing lipsticks.

The body of a lipstick is a mixture of castor oil and wax, generally beeswax or carnauba wax (popular as a car wax because of its high melting point, 85°C). The aim is to have a mixture that is thixotropic (like tomato sauce)—that is it should remain stiff in the tube but flow easily when under the pressure of applying it to the lips. Esters such as 2-propyl myristate (14 carbon carboxylic acid) are added to reduce 'stickiness' and improve the flow across the lips.

Algin, which is extracted from seaweed, holds water and

Lipstick sticks

The principal of a small middle school had a problem with a few older girls using lipstick. After applying it in the bathroom they would press their lips to the mirror and leave lip prints.

To end the practice he gathered together all the girls who wore lipstick and told them he wanted to meet with them in the ladies' room at 2.00pm. They arrived on time and found the principal and the school custodian waiting for them.

The principal explained what a job it was for the custodian to clean the mirror every night. He said he felt the girls did not fully understand this and he wanted to show them just how hard the lipstick was to clean.

The custodian then demonstrated. He took a long-handled brush out of a box. He dipped the brush in the nearest toilet, then moved to the mirror and proceeded to remove the lipstick.

That was the last day the girls pressed their lips on the mirror!

allows the plant to survive tidal rise and fall. It has been used for 30 years as a moisturising ingredient in lipstick. Better extraction techniques now keep the algin close to original, and the lipstick should last for days instead of hours. A special cleaner (mainly salt and alcohol) is needed to remove residual pigment from the skin.

Reference

A great source of technical information on cosmetics can be found in the 930 pages of 'Harry's Cosmeticology', 7th ed., edited by J.B. Wilkinson and R.J. Moore, Chemical Publishing Co, NY 1982.

Perfumes—are you being conned?

PERFUME COMES FROM the Latin *per* ('through') and *fume* ('smoke'). The first perfumers were priests who burned resins, leaves and wood as incense. They believed that the sweet-smelling smoke carried their prayers to the gods. The Egyptians were probably the first to use perfumes in their private lives; Cleopatra ordered the sails of her barge be drenched with cyprinum in order to attract Mark Antony. When the crusaders returned to Europe they brought new fragrances such as musk, citrus, jasmine and sandalwood. The peak in the passion for perfumes was reached by Louis XV in his eighteenth-century royal courts.

Perfumes consist of essential oils (from 'essence') generally concentrated in the petals of the flowers, but they can occur elsewhere. Peeling an orange releases tiny droplets of a sweet-smelling oil located just beneath the orange's skin.

The essential oils generally belong to a group of chemicals called terpenes. The main component of terpentine is alpha-pinene. (Mineral turpentine, or turps, is a petroleum fraction similar to kerosene which is used as a substitute.) Terpenes tend to be soluble in both fat and alcohol, but these two materials are not themselves very soluble in each other and the alcohol and liquid fat will form two layers. The Egyptians learnt to steep petals in warm liquid fat to dissolve out the terpenes, a process called maceration. The petals were changed regularly, and when the fat was saturated with terpene, it was shaken up with alcohol. The perfume moved from the liquid fat layer to the alcohol layer, a process called extraction. Because the warm fat decomposes some of the more sensitive components, the French developed a gentler process called enfleurage.

In this, glass plates are coated with purified fat and petals laid on them, then the plates are placed in an enclosed chamber. Again the petals are replaced every few days. The fat is scraped off the plates and the oils extracted with alcohol. This is then concentrated by distilling off some of the alcohol, providing floral absolute.

Steam distillation was used to make rose water, the first real perfume, in the eleventh century, and is still used for most oils, including rose, spice and mint oils, sometimes under vacuum for more sensitive oils (see p. 59). The best citrus oils are produced by rupturing the oil glands in the peel and not allowing this oil to come in contact with the juice. Synthetics dominate the market today, although the really top-quality perfumes still rely on many natural extracts.

John Lambeth, perfumer at Dragoco (Sydney), led me through his lovely library of rows of compactus full of valuable little bottles. These bottles are not just about pretty smells, but are the raw products of his trade. According to Lambeth, you match the perfume to the product. You ask yourself, 'What are the trends? What is the market? What are the demographics?' The type of 'new car smell' used to sell old lemons is designed to match the prospective buyer. What works for a Ford may be quite unsuitable for a Porsche. Natural is in and the levels of active ingredient used are now lower than previously.

With a fruit flavour, the question is, at what stage in the 'ripeness' is the smell of fruit 'correct'? In the fruit it changes continuously and the traditional 'expected' smell often corresponds to over-ripe. Chemicals used include p-hydroxy phenyl butanone (raspberry ketone), eugenol methyl ether (from Huon pine) and Bulgarian lavender oil. Rosemary extracted by liquid carbon dioxide, smells very close to the plant from which it was extracted. Two and a half tonnes of fresh garden peas were processed by Keith Murray (CSIRO) to extract one drop of essence (pyrazines) to which your nose is instantly fatigued. This means within a very short time you can no longer smell the essence. (Nice while it lasts, though.) Murray did this to see what it was that gave peas (and their shells) that distinctive flavour. It was a potential high value perfume component.

I 'know' that smell but can't picture it! You need to 'see' a smell. Without a visual image it is often hard to recognise a perfume—a rose laced with lavender will seem to smell like a rose because that's what you see. Most flowers stop making perfume after being picked. Tuberoses are an exception. So perfume design is an art with some science.

A perfume is designed in terms of three 'notes'. The top notes, the citrus and fresh components, are volatile and evaporate quickly. The middle notes are slower and include jasmine, violet and rose components—the florals. The base notes are slow to evaporate and are woody, mossy, musky and amber notes. These notes are described in terms of a triangle with the small amount of the most volatile material at the top. Try spotting perfumes onto smelling strips (blotting paper) and smelling at various intervals. The top note comes off in the first minutes. Smelling again in fifteen minutes will reveal the middle notes. Smell again in 30 minutes and further components will be revealed and the base may still be evident a few days later.

The ever popular Eau de Cologne 4711 is just top note (lemon, orange, bergamot, rosemary). The name comes from the house number where it was made. When Napoleon occupied Köln in 1792, his troops bought up supplies for the hot road ahead.

Some modern perfumes use a monolithic block. For example, Tresor uses four ingredients to make up 80 per cent of the perfume and Stephanie uses one ingredient to make up 50 per cent of the perfume. Methyl octin carbonate (methyl 2-nonynoate) evokes the smell of violets and motorcycles: Dior's Fahrenheit uses a lot of it. Coumarin, the primary ingredient of Cacherel's Lulu, is the characteristic smell of late summer, from whose flowers and grasses it is actually derived.

Orris butter, a complex derivative of the roots of the iris, is vaguely floral in small amounts, but obscenely fleshy (like the smell beneath a breast) in quantity. Whales vomit ambergris. It floats on the surface to be transformed by sunlight. The musk deer is farmed in China. Because tonnes of musk are needed each year, it is now mostly synthetic. (Remember those pink musk sweets we had as kids? They were probably quite toxic.)

The civet cat is kept in cages in Ethiopia and its glands are scraped. The concentrate smells like skatole, the major odour component of human faeces (hope they have scraped in the right place!). It is amazingly sexy in subliminal doses. It features in Guerlain's Jicky, introduced in 1889, and probably the first modern perfume (and one whose market has changed over 100 years—it now has a following by gay men). Chanel No. 5 was launched in 1923 with a synthetic 'aldehyde' base and is still very popular. The Americans challenged French dominance in 1953, when Estee Lauder introduced Youth Dew, dropping delicate floral for a powerful oriental scent. Revlon's Charlie in 1972 was for the liberated woman who bought her own perfume, and Giorgi in 1984 was the first perfume to be advertised in scent strips in magazines.

UK specialist aroma producer, Fred Dale of Air Products of Blackpool, has been supplying museums, theme parks and shops with custom-made aromas like gun smoke, cut grass, smell of dinosaurs and South African Zulu warriors (with a little poetic licence). He is looking to use smells to help the blind, for example, in a shopping centre, using a pine aroma outside toilets and floral aroma outside lifts. At Christmas 1995, unsuspecting passers by were lured into the Tate Gallery with the smell of brandy and into Woolworths with the smell of mulled wine.

John Lambeth has a brilliant 'rainforest smell' commissioned by the army of a country to our north to mask the odour of their jungle troops.

'You do not have to dabble for very long to realise that the world of smell has no reliable maps, no single language, no comprehensible metaphorical structure within which we might comprehend it and navigate around it' (Brian Eno, Visiting Professor, Royal College of Art). The best we can do with smells is to make comparisons. Karanal is like 'striking a flint', aldehyde C_{14} is 'like peach skins', beta ionine is 'like latex'.

'Perhaps our sense of belonging to a world held together by networks of ephemeral confidences (such as philosophies and stock markets) rather than permanent certainties, predisposes us to embrace the pleasures of our most primitive, unlanguaged sense', says Eno. 'Being mystified does not frighten us as much as it used to. And the point for me is not to expect perfumery to take its place in some nice, reliable, rational world order, but to expect everything else to become like it; the future will be like a perfume.'

Ever wondered why Christian Dior's Poison comes in a dark bottle? Perhaps to give it a poisonous ambience? Maybe. More mundanely and more likely it is to hide the fact that the colour changes in time, a no-no for most consumer products, particularly cosmetics. With time, a so-called Schiff's base is formed from the reaction of an amine with a carbonyl but this has no effect on the fragrance or the colour on the skin. Likewise there is no skin colour change with Elizabeth Taylor's Passion, which is actually dark blue in the bottle.

Sense of smell

In order to have a scent, a molecule must evaporate reasonably efficiently. This means the molecule must not be too large; a molecular mass under 300 daltons is usual. The molecule must also be able to bind to the scent receptors which, in humans, are found deep within the nose and cover an area about the size of a postage stamp. Although humans have a poor sense of smell compared with other mammals, most of us can identify a strawberry, say, which is a complex mixture of about 300 components with a total amount of around 10 parts per million in the berry. Chemists use a large, slow, complex machine called a gas chromatograph to do the same job.

In September 1986, *National Geographic* carried out a large smell survey. Around 1.5 million people from all over the world were tested with six scents using 'scratch and sniff' sheets. The six scents were androstenone (a steroid from the fat of boars, released—in modified form—when the boar drools after sexual arousal), eugenol (oil of cloves), galaxolide (synthetic musk), isoamyl acetate (the main component in banana scent) and mercaptan (a smelly sulfur compound added to odourless natural gas as a warning agent). While women performed better than men, only half the sample group could smell all six scents. Some 1.2 per cent of the respondents could not smell any of the scents! Androstenone, found also in very low levels in human male sweat, and mooted as a possible human sex attractant, was smelled by the fewest number, and these described it very differently. However, it has found a commercial use as an aerosol spray in assessing sows for artificial insemination programs.

Aromatherapy is based on the premise that scents affect moods and emotion at a deep level. There is even one patent published for a product that is claimed to prompt people to pay when they receive their bill! Sniff the bookmark and buy this book.

Hair-raising physics!

WE 'NAKED APES' have about 150 000 individual hairs, each about 70 micrometres in diameter, the same as our chimpanzee cousins. However, ours are fine and short rather than furry.

The growth of scalp hair is complex and fascinating. The growing phase lasts about six years in women and three to four years in men. The length attained if uncut is 70 to 80 centimetres in women and 40 to 50 centimetres in men. The growth then ceases and roots develop attaching the hair to the follicle. The follicle shrivels and rests for three to six months, then starts to produce a new hair, which pushes the old one out. One hundred mature hairs are pushed out every day (four years for a complete male-head turnover) and 90 per cent of the hairs are actively growing at any one time.

The cuticle protects the hair shaft by forming a sheath around it. If a hair is cut, the cement that holds the overlapping cells together oozes out and seals the end. The structure of the hair shaft is a complex yarn (literally). Consisting of a tangle of keratin protein chains imbedded in a protein matrix. Five of these threads twist together to form a yarn. The yarn, in turn, is bundled into cables. A single hair will support a mass of about 80 grams. So, if the hairs did not pull out, a mere thousand (less than 1% of the scalp) could support a person weighing 80 kilograms!

The pigment melanin, which gives skin its colour, also colours hair. Different amounts of the same pigment and in different places account for light blonde to blue-black. Only redheads are different in that their hair contains an additional unique iron-based pigment, which indeed makes their hair 'rusty'.

A hairy tale

The strong bonding of metals by the sulfur group on the protein in hair creates an interesting forensic possibility. The metal content of a particular section of hair reflects the metal intake of the person at the time when that section of hair was actively growing. A classic historical case relates to the death of Napoleon in 1821 in (his second) exile on the island of St Helena. Examination of his hair at a later date showed significant levels of arsenic, and the position on the hair gave an approximate date of exposure. Arsenic was a common component in dyes used for the popular green wallpapers of the time and microbes digesting the paper could disperse the arsenic into the surroundings. There is no need for a deliberate poisoning hypothesis.

The condition or gloss of hair depends on the outer cuticle, whose stacked transparent plates reflect the light. Too much chemical treatment, too much heat and excessive brushing dislodge the protective tiles, reduce reflection and give that dull appearance seen in the 'before' part of advertisements for hair products. The raised scales can catch one another and cause tangles, while the escape of moisture from the cortex causes the hair to appear dry and brittle.

The basic aim of all hair conditioners is to smooth the surface of the hair and thereby avoid all the other negative effects. While cationic surfactants were the original conditioners, these have been replaced by silicone-based conditioners, which are extremely good lubricants for hair. The displacement of moisture on the surface allows hair to dry more quickly, the same trick is used for waterproofing camping and wet-weather gear. When you feel the treated hair, you are really feeling silicone. The reduction in friction also reduces static, and thus 'fly-away hair'.

Making your hair darker is relatively easy, particularly if you don't mind doing it fairly often. Semipermanent rinses and washes all share the property of attaching the colour to the outside of the hair. The bright fashion colours use large granules, which vanish with one washing. The finer particles of more traditional rinses bond to the scales of the cuticle and survive many shampooings.

With permanent dyeing, the idea is to move through the cuticle and enter the deeper cortex cells. Hydrogen peroxide is used to soften the cortex and thus allow very small granules to pass through. It also bleaches the melanin and so allows lighter shades. Thirdly its oxidation action clumps the granules in the cortex and thus hinders their migration out again. Hydrogen peroxide probably weakens the hair in the longer term. A popular preparation for camouflaging stray grey hairs works by depositing a layer of metal salts only on the hair surface that do not enter the hair shaft. The metal tarnishes or reacts with sulfur in the keratin (hair protein) to give a dull green-black result of dubious merit. Lead is most common, but silver, copper, iron, nickel, cobalt and even bismuth salts are used. (See also p. 189.)

Using natural vegetable dyes has again become fashionable. Henna comes from dried, powdered leaves of *Lawsonia*, removed before flowering. It owes its dyeing properties to a derivative of naphthaquinone called *lawsone*, which works in hot acidic solution. Washed hair is packed with a paste of henna and citric (or similar) acid for a time varying anything from five to 60 minutes, depending on the shade required and the quality of henna and condition of the hair. It is messy to use (it will stain the keratin of finger nails as well as hair), limited in colour range and repeated use tends to spoil some of the effect giving a hard auburn colour. However, henna deposits inside the hair shaft and so the colour is stable, and it is non-toxic and non-sensitising.

The chemistry of adjusting the curl falls into groups depending on the degree of permanency required. The simplest procedure is to wet the hair, which protonates and breaks some of the disulfide bonds holding the proteins in shape. Drying the hair while it is held in either a straighter or curlier shape than before sets it temporarily. Indeed even heat alone on dry hair causes some changes. The slightest increase in humidity causes the hair to revert to its normal style. This sensitivity of hair curl to heat and humidity is the basis of the picturesque 'weather houses' in which two figures balanced on a horizontal axle are suspended on a (human) hair. The changing weather conditions twist the hair, which causes the figures to move in and out of a doorway.

Attack by sulfur bond breaking chemicals on the internal proteins of hair makes the hair floppy, allowing it to be set. The effect is neutralised with peroxide, the hair is then held in its new shape. Incidentally, depilatory creams and lotions work on the same principle and with the same ingredients. They soften and loosen the unwanted hair, which is then easily removed.

Combing

Too much friction when combing hair pulls the skin, but too little makes the hair feel greasy. It is the friction between the hair fibres, not between the hair and comb, which is important for easy combing.

When the hair is wet, it can contain about one-third of its mass in water. This water drags hair fibres together. With frizzy and very curly hair, there is less opportunity for drawing together, and such hair is about three times easier to comb wet than dry, exactly the opposite to straight hair. Chemically straightened or permed hair can radically change this behaviour.

Can armpits hide more
than watermelons?

MOST ANTIPERSPIRANTS ARE based on aluminium aqueous (chloro) complexes, and these have been evaluated for performance in agonising detail with all possible techniques under every conceivable condition. Aluminium and zirconium compounds are all that is left in the market to stop perspiration, after the whole of Mendeleyev's Masterpiece (the periodic table of the chemical elements) has been tried and rejected. It is not that other salts don't work, they do, and include the common: copper, iron and tin; the obvious: lanthanum and cerium (being relatives of aluminium); and the esoteric: samarium and praseodymium. Unfortunately, with these, while people perspired less, they expired more. Deaths, for some reason, tend to provoke customer resistance!

Aluminium salts appear to work by producing an insoluble hydroxide gel in the sweat pores and thus blocking them. Numerous tests show that the aluminium does not cross the skin barrier and enter the body so that this source cannot be accused of contributing to the body load and the possibility of Alzheimer's disease.

If 70 per cent of the world's scientists work for the military, then most of the others must work for cosmetic companies. This is not surprising when we are told that in 1986, sales of deodorant soaps, antiperspirants and deodorants made up approximately 14 per cent of the $8.6 billion spent in the United States on health and beauty aids.

Perspiration was first effectively controlled by Mum (circa 1888) which contained zinc oxide (now used as a sunscreen).

Sniffy!

The 18th century essayist Samuel Johnson once corrected the English grammar of a woman complaining about his bodily odours with the retort: 'Lady, you smell, I stink.'

This neutralised the smelly acids and helped kill bacteria. In 1895 came Lifebouy containing cresylic acid. It smelled like phenol (Dettol) and replaced one unpleasant odour with another. In 1948 came Dial with hexachlorophene, and this antibacterial survived until a French firm in 1972 inadvertently put a level of 6 per cent into a baby powder that then caused over 30 deaths.

Sweat glands can be divided into two types, eccrine (E) and aprocine (A). The Es are stimulated by heat and help cool us down. The As are triggered by emotion and cause copious flow in embarrassing circumstances (for instance, when on a lie detector). As are found on palms and soles. Es are found everywhere else. The armpits (called axillae in polite texts) have both.

If all the approximately three million sweat glands on our bodies worked at full bore, so to speak, we would produce about 10 litres of sweat per day. Each armpit (sorry, axillary vault) has about 25 000 sweat glands, and it takes only ten minutes to produce 1.5 millilitres of sweat after an emotional stimulus. You can see why there is an annual $1.5 billion market for anti-perspirants in the United States alone.

Microbiologists love studying the axillae because their 'semi-occluded anatomy is less prone to environmental contamination'. Apparently it is hard to miss the microbes because they crowd the pit at a million to the square centimetre. An initial study has shown that there is no statistically significant difference between the left and right armpit, or between left and right handers, or between males and females. There is, however, a big difference between those who wash and those who don't. The variety and names of the microbes suggest to a non-microbiologist that they must be a pretty ferocious lot.

Bacteria work on the secretions to produce the odours. Let me quote: 'Axillary odour is a mixture of many 'notes'

Ode(our)

Once upon a time (in 50 BC), Catullus wrote a poem that foreshadowed the modern theory that microbes are responsible for body odours. The poem has been freely translated as follows:

An ugly rumour harms your reputation.
Underneath your arms they say you keep a fierce goat which alarms all comers—and no wonder,
for the least Beauty would never bed with rank beast.
So either kill the pest that makes the stink
Or else stop wondering why the women shrink.

[a technical term used in the chemical perfumery industry], with the dominating notes identified as isovaleric acid and 5–andost–16–en–3–one and 5–andost–16–en–3–ol'. Isovaleric acid gives the armpit its sweaty odour. The latter two unpronounceables are formed from body steroids, and the last is variously described as smelling like stale urine or worse. They probably do wonders for the microbe's sporting prowess. Another armpit steroid with a natural musk odour gained notoriety by being added to a perfume (Andron). However, there were no sex-attractant effects found that could be reliably repeated.

The hircine (L. goat-like) smell referred to in Catullus's poem (box) is due to another compound present in the armpits, 4-ethyloctanoic acid. Mature female goats in oestrus respond specifically to this compound, so when in range, keep your arms down unless you want an unusual experience.

Naturally, the cosmetics industry has poured millions of dollars into seeing whether this response can be replicated in more affluent females. Humans can smell this acid at 1.8 parts per billion, one of the lowest thresholds for any compound. Unfortunately, human females find it disagreeable. Nevertheless, experiments have been done on 'cognitive evaluation of sexual stimuli' (viewing porn photos) under the influence of each of these chemicals to see whether they change male or female responses. Some very interesting results have been obtained . . .

Widely published, on the other hand, is the experiment in which extracts of female axillary odour using ethanol extracts of armpit sweat on pads were placed on the upper lips of female subjects. These were found to cause the menstrual cycles of the subjects to approach that of the donor. This suggests that the well-established synchronisation of the menstrual cycles of women living in close proximity is mediated chemically by sweat compounds.

Extracts from males appear to have a mild regularisation effect on aberrant-length menstrual cycles (shorter than 26 or longer than 33 days). This could be biologically significant in that fertility is correlated with normal-length cycles (29.5 days, give or take three days). We must always be thankful for the initiatives of industrial research, regardless of the original motives.

When the times are tough and the road is long, it helps to remember what the Armenians say: 'The watermelon will not ripen in your armpit.' Just what chemistry had the Armenians discovered?

Reference

Antiperspirants and Deodorants, eds K. Laden & C. B. Felger, in Cosmetic Science and Technology Series No. 7, Marcel Dekker, NY 1988.

Can you test a sunscreen in your urine?

WE CAN'T REALLY see the sun! Sunlight is only a very narrow range selected by our eyes from the huge span of radiation poured out by the sun into the space which bathes us. We can think of the visible range we see as a single 'octave' of this immense output. Indeed, the frequency, or 'pitch', of the violet light is roughly twice that of the red light. A musical term is appropriate because both light and sound come in waves.

Pushing the musical analogy, the music of less than one hand's span on a piano keyboard is all our eyes perceive of the full spectrum. We would have difficulty in appreciating a full orchestra with only this narrow limited band of information. A radio receiver's view of the sun provides a very different moving picture from our visible one. A bee's utraviolet view of the surroundings is quite different to ours.

But other octaves—infrared and ultraviolet, X-rays and even microwaves—can affect us elsewhere on our bodies, and indeed excess can damage us, but the information they provide is limited to warmth and burning sensations, generally too late. Too much ultraviolet light damages the hereditary material in the cell (DNA). DNA provides a genetic code using four chemical bases, CGAT. Ultraviolet light can fuse two bases together into a dimer in the cells of the skin and cause misreading of the code with consequent health dangers including cancer.

Normal human skin cells have an enzyme system which can repair ultraviolet damage by excising the dimers and closing the gap, but only so often. A rare genetic disease in which this enzyme is lacking makes its sufferers very liable to skin cancer because the dimer changes the DNA code in the skin cells.

The natural skin colour of humans evolved to match the intensity of sunlight according to the region of the earth in which they evolved. However, with mass movement of peoples, this neat balance has been upset: pale skins in sunny climates suffer from sunburn and increased skin cancer, while dark skins in unsunny climates have problems caused by insufficient vitamin D synthesis in the skin. Women who wear veils and the traditional black robes of the hijab, can also suffer this deficiency.

For most of recorded history, white skin implied a lofty position in society. While workers, serfs and slaves spent most of their time in the sun, aristocrats sought shade by carrying parasols, wearing hats and sun bonnets and staying indoors. However, the industrial revolution did away with the pursuit of pallor. Workers, herded into factories, spent long hours indoors. Shade became cheap while sunlight was expensive. A suntan showed that its wearers had the wealth and leisure time to travel to places where they could get a lot of sun.

Tanning is nature's way of controlling the level of sunlight activity on the skin by providing a natural block. The tanning of our skin involves a pigment called melanin. We are all born with different amounts of it. Fair-skinned people have a little, olive-complexioned people have more, and black people have a lot. Melanin reacts to the sun in two stages. In the first stage, pale (unoxidised) melanin granules near our skin's surface are changed by ultraviolet light to their dark brown (oxidised) form. This gives an immediate tan, usually within an hour. It fades within a day. A more lasting tan results from the second stage. In this process, new quantities of melanin are produced from tyrosine, an abundant amino acid in our skin's protein. This second stage tan endures for several days without further exposure. Additional sunbathing not only produces more melanin but also deepens its colour (the polymer chain lengthens).

However, the final effect of ultraviolet radiation is damage to the proteins that make up the skin's connective and elastic tissue. This leads to irreversible wrinkled, leathery and sagging skin. The word 'tanning' for the effect of sun on skin is well chosen.

There are formulations that induce a suntan-like darker skin without sunlight. The tan is artificial because no melanin is involved in the process and the browning offers no protection against sunburn. Such a brown complexion is formed through a reaction with the skin protein by the products active ingredient (usually dihydroxyacetone). It is interesting that glass does not transmit much light with wavelength below 350 nanometres— the dangerous range for people. If you sunbake behind a window, the main effect is reddening of the skin by heating. The same is not true of plastics, which can transmit light of shorter wavelengths.

Of the three types of skin cancer, the least common but most dangerous is melanoma. Deaths from melanoma in Australia have increased since the 1920s, and its victims are often professional or managerial workers, not workers who spend their days in the sun. In Queensland, one new case of melanoma occurs each year for every 6000 inhabitants. In cloudier Britain the incidence rate is one new case per year per 37 000 people. The Queensland rate is 50 per cent higher than in the United States, where nearly 20 000 will be diagnosed with the disease this year and more than half of these will die from it (mainly men).

Women in Australia develop melanomas mainly on the legs, while in men they occur anywhere. The rare instances of melanoma in dark-skinned people tend to be on the palms of the hands or soles of the feet. While increased exposure to sunlight increases the likelihood of melanoma, the cancerous growth does not necessarily occur on the parts of the body actually exposed to the sunlight.

No-one knows why these marked differences occur. For melanoma (but not other skin cancers), the damage appears to be transmitted via chemical messengers from the point of exposure to other parts of the body. Because it takes years before cancer appears, exposure early in life is the most crucial factor. Office workers who might get short bursts of excessive exposure intermittently (on weekends and holidays) appear at least as susceptible as outdoor workers continuously exposed.

We have tended to get things wrong about our Chernobyl in the sky. While protecting ourselves against excess sun is very important, the hole in the ozone layer will have no practical impact on skin cancer rates. The reason is as follows: The American National Academy of Sciences has found that your chance of getting skin cancer increases by 1 per cent every

10 kilometres you move towards the equator. It also estimates that a 1 per cent decrease in ozone (in the ozone layer) increases your chance of skin cancer by 2 per cent. So even if, as some doomsday scientists have predicted, the ozone hole increases UV rays by 10 per cent, that would be equivalent to swimming for the same length of time at Bondi Beach rather than at Wollongong, 100 kilometres to the south.

Sun damages hair as well as skin; the tryptophan degrades, disulfide bonds are broken and the hair surface gets rougher.

Except for the immediate short-lived tanning response, it is not possible to screen selectively for true tanning while protecting against sunburn and skin cancer. Darkening pigmentation requires preceding sunburn (which can be kept at a low level) to trigger the process. Sunscreens are used to lower the dose of light received by the skin to the point where tanning may have a chance to catch up to the burning.

Sunscreens that are formulated to give a quick tan but to suppress sunburn (and true tanning) will absorb light better in the 290–320 nanometre wavelength (UVB) range than in the longer wavelength range (UVA). Problems with allergies from PABA (p-aminobenzoates) have led to its replacement by many other organic actives. Inorganic materials such as ultra-fine zinc oxide powders provide non-allergenic alternatives.

By reducing the size of the zinc oxide particle from the normal 250 nanometres (billionth of a metre) to 10 nanometres, about 1000 times smaller than the diameter of a human hair, CSIRO has produced a new screen, Sunsorb, which spreds more uniformly on the skin, is fairly transparent to visible light so it can be used in moisturisers and make-up, but still scatters UV backwards away from the skin.

Some organic substances may enter the bloodstream by passing through the skin (see p. 23). Not many actually stay in the skin itself in spite of advertising claims of the cosmetic industry. Assume the total skin area of an adult is around 1 square metre. This area needs about 30 millilitres or 30 grams of sunscreen (six teaspoons) for an effective screen. Assume that a screen has an active concentration of 150 milligrams per gram of lotion. Then about 4.5 grams of active lotion will be deposited on the skin. Not a trivial amount of any chemical with the potential to be absorbed into the bloodstream. Indeed, when sunscreens containing benzoate or salicylates are applied to the skin, these chemicals can be detected within 30 minutes in the urine of the user. Those people who need to avoid salicylates in food should also avoid absorption of them from sunscreens.

I chaired a committee that deliberated for six years and finally set an Australian standard for sunscreens, AS 2604 in 1983 (modified as AS/NZ in 1997). The complexities of devising a reliable, yet not too expensive test for a sunscreen are hard to imagine. What is most important is that an adequate amount of sunscreen be used. There were wildly different results between laboratory measurements of UV absorption and measurements from real life exposure. It was the latter that was finally used to set the sun protection factor on labels, SPF 2–15.

What does SPF (sun protection factor) really mean? If your unprotected white skin shows the first sign of reddening after ten minutes in the midday sun (typical), then a properly applied screen with SPF of 15 increases this time by ten, to between two to three hours. In 1997, claims of up to 30+ were allowed to be made by manufacturers. In theory, with an SPF of 30, protection should last four to six hours. In practice, the screen needs to be replenished every few hours, so the increase in label from 15 to 30+ was something I refused in 1983, but is now accepted.

Quality of screen is determined mainly by how long the screen stays spread uniformly over the skin. A sunscreen must be chemically and photochemically stable, otherwise its absorption ability changes with time. It must be soluble in the cosmetic base but insoluble in water or perspiration. An upper limit to claims for the rate the screen washes off in water—water resistance—were also set by the standards committee in 1983. Fresh water dissolves sunscreen more effectively than salt water.

Because of the importance of adequate application of sunscreens, I argued strongly for the availability to the consumer of large packs at moderate cost. This call was answered at the time (1980s) by the large supermarket chains and more recently by the Cancer Council.

The sunscreen standard is now enforced by law in Australia, which means you can buy on price knowing that performance as a screen is guaranteed. The composition of actives varies considerably so you can then select for personal skin sensitivities and allergies, or image. One of the things we learnt in devising

Alexander's Ragtime Band

The story is told that Alexander the Great made use of the fact that some colours are photochemically unstable and bleach rapidly in sunlight. Because his commanders didn't have watches to synchronise their attacks, he gave them bleachable coloured rags to put around their arms so that they could measure time during the day. Thus came into being Alexander's Ragtime Band!

the standard was that female sensitivity to sunlight varied enormously during the monthly cycle and so the SPF testing is all done on male backs. Thus the type and strength you (women) need, may have to be varied. Try different brands.

Like voting, apply sunscreens early and often.

Are sunplastics trustworthy?

PATHETIC ISN'T IT? The Australian Taxation Office (ATO) has twice been beaten in the Federal Court in its attempts at preventing outdoor workers from claiming sunglasses as tax deductions, while other parts of the same Government encourage their use. Excessive ultraviolet and infrared radiation can cause eye damage. But the ATO in its wisdom argues that, unlike other protective gear, sunglasses complying with the Australian Standard are not specifically designed for occupational protection.

While hats provide the best protection against the sun, for those who don't wear them, sunglasses provide the next best answer. A deliberate decision was made in devising the standard that general purpose sunglasses needed to give wide protection including for outdoor workers. There was a need for specific purpose sunglasses, but only for very particular situations. There was no reason why worker protection shouldn't also be fashionable.

Devising the standard actually all started in the Southlands shopping centre in Canberra in 1978. A conscientious pharmacist was measuring some simple optical properties of sunglasses and noticed widely different UV absorption rates between left- and right-hand lenses; some had faded in the shop window, and one pair cut out visible light more than ultraviolet (UV)! Brand name was no protection. A very expensive French brand was one of the worst performers. More sophisticated measurements carried out in the chemistry department at the Australian

National University confirmed his results and these were published by Canberra Consumers in September 1978.

Problems arose when 'glasses' were replaced by 'plastics'. The two common plastic materials used were polycarbonate and acrylic (perspex). These do not absorb ultraviolet or infrared as well as glass. The pupil of the eye opens up in response to a reduction in intensity of visible light, caused by absorption of light by the plastic sunglass lens. However, if the plastic cuts back disproportionately less ultraviolet or infrared radiation than it does visible light, the overall exposure of the eye lens (and retina) to those radiations will be increased. The eye protects itself quite adequately in normal sunlight if no sunglasses are worn through the pupils' contracting to reduce light.

The defects discovered in sunglasses prompted some action. Standards Australia was in a consumer protection mood when we sat down with industry, academia, CSIRO, government and other reps to set standards for sunglasses—and sunscreens for good measure. Consumer group reps often chaired these committees, and I found these people a wonderful source of reliable but unpublished information. Meetings dragged on over six years, and pleasant hours were wasted arguing such things as whether wearing sunglasses while driving at night was a hazard. (It can be for highly coloured glasses and when the wearer is colour blind because the glasses may distort colour perception.)

There is little point in setting standards unless they are either enforced or the public is strongly encouraged to use them. With children's bike helmets the tactic was to make them 'cool'. Ugly, clumsy products were replaced by streamlined and colourful fashion items. Wearing them was self-enforced through peer group pressure. With sunglasses, the optical needs of outdoor workers and casual wearers are similar. Only exposure to excess UV and IR that you might get from arc welding, lasers, skiing and some water sports, for example, need extra light absorbing requirements. So why not encourage macho outdoor workers with a protective fashion accessory as well? Hence, the common standard general use and outdoor workers AS 1067, which also defines the quality of the optics to prevent distortion of shapes or colours.

The sunglass standard was made mandatory soon after its

Disco light

The UV light emitted by the mercury fluorescent lamps used in discos occurs at 365 nanometres, a rate which is absorbed by most sunglasses but is beyond the range absorbed by sunscreens. Fluorescors used in white cotton shirts (and detergents used to wash them) absorb the UV light, which is re-emitted as blue light. (Fluorescors are added to make pale yellow cotton look whiter than white in sunlight.) The lens of the eye reacts the same way as these fluorescors. The lens absorbs the UV light and emits it again as diffuse blue light. This directionless light is picked up by the retina and so these disco lights appear fuzzy when you look at them. It is believed that no damage is done to the eyes by this particular (365 nanometres) UV light.

The quartz halogen lamp operates at a higher temperature than conventional globes and produces ultraviolet radiation which its quartz envelope lets out. In the midday summer sun, the recommended daily exposure for UV is reached in about fifteen minutes. At 25 centimetres' distance (one foot), a 50 watt quartz halogen globe without filter can deliver the same amount of UV in about fifteen minutes. This increases to 40 minutes at 50 centimetres, two hours 40 minutes at 100 centimetres, and a full working day at 175 centimetres (inverse square law).

publication, so it doesn't matter where you buy your sunglasses, at an optometrist, general store or the markets, they must comply. (Fashion and toy glasses do not have to comply.) The regulator, the Australian Competition and Consumer Commission (ACCC), tests products regularly, and even top brands occasionally fail, generally for their labelling.

The Australian Cancer Association/Polaroid sunglasses give good protection around the sides and top as well as directly through the lens. Polaroid is colour neutral and gives added comfort by cutting down reflected glare from flat horizontal surfaces like water and snow, because reflected light is polarised in one (horizontal) direction and the Polaroid in the glasses is orientated to transmit vertically polarised light and absorbs this reflected glare strongly. One Cancer Council/Polaroid design fits over prescription glasses.

Australia was the first country to set many of these standards, which have since been adopted overseas. The standards-setting process was by consensus, and those manufacturers participating do so on a voluntary basis.

Further Information

For more on sunglasses look at *Choice* magazine for October 1999.

IN AND OUT OF THE OFFICE

Why leave condoms
on the copier

I DON'T EXPECT many of you would deliberately leave a condom on the photocopier machine! (Except, of course, as an occupational health and safety measure.) So why would that be?

The market for natural rubber collapsed after the Second World War because of the boom in synthetic rubber developed for military vehicles. But natural rubber still has some unmatched attractive properties that make it useful for rubber bands, surgeon's gloves and the above unmentionables. It is used wherever thin or sensitive disposable products are needed. However, natural rubber is very sensitive to attack by ozone.

Ozone (O_3) is formed from the stable, friendly oxygen you breathe (O_2) by ultraviolet light or electrical discharge. It consists of three oxygen atoms in a (bent) row and is very poisonous.

Despite the fact that ozone at ground level is normally found at concentrations of less than 0.1 parts per million, it is the primary agent for the deterioration of rubber. Rubber molecules share with vegetable oils the property of being 'unsaturated', that is they contain double bonds between carbon atoms and these bonds are susceptible to attack. Polyunsaturated vegetable oils have lots of these bonds which are attacked by oxygen and form a tough surface solid layer—a necessary property used in the old oil paints and varnishes, but undesirable in the kitchen or in an oil lamp. (See pp. 66–7 on anti-oxidants.)

While natural rubber is unfazed by oxygen, it is attacked by even small amounts of ozone. Stretching rubber induces microscopic cracks and breaks, opening up further rubber surface for attack. Ozone breaks apart the long chain molecules and also

Bleached sugar flowers

To keep cut flowers in bloom longer, dissolve half a tablespoon of sugar and one teaspoon of bleach in about half a litre of water. Apparently, the effect of the preservative is most marked on carnations (which have been kept this way as long as three weeks), and roses. Freesias also last longer, but don't use it on chrysanthemums which keep fairly well anyway.

Reason? Sugar is a food and bleach kills bacteria which can block the channels in the stem.

increases the cross-links between the chains. This means the rubber becomes less elastic and won't even stretch any more, becomes much weaker and finally breaks at a touch. The rubber has *perished* prematurely.

Photocopiers use discharge lamps that emit untraviolet light and also produce ozone just as sunlight and lightning produce it in the upper atmosphere. Excess ozone from unventilated copiers can act as a powerful respiratory irritant. A stretched (or more slowly, unstretched) natural rubber band or condom left near a machine will soon perish. Hey presto, an excellent test of the machine's ozone output.

There is a lot more you can do with a rubber band and the like. Hang one up and clip a weight on the end to stretch it. Now warm the band with a hair dryer. It *shrinks* on heating and gets tougher. Exactly the opposite to metals and other solids, which expand on heating.

Or you can stretch a band quickly and touch your lips to it. It feels hot. If you leave it stretched for a while to cool down to room temperature again, and then suddenly let it contract, it will feel cold on the lips.

The reason is that the long molecules of rubber like to be curled up and stretching makes them line up unnaturally. The energy put in by stretching comes out as heat. That is why you find after a fast stretch, the rubber feels hot to the lips. If, on the other hand, you *put heat in* (from the haidryer), the rubber wants to curl up more, and becomes shorter and stiffer. Conversely, rubber car tyres on a really cold morning have had heat taken out of them overnight, thus becoming more stretched and less elastic. When you drive off, the flattened bottom of the tyre can stay with you and give a very clunky ride until the tyre heats up.

It is the nature of rubber, with its long polymer molecules that want to be curled up, that makes it expand and contract with heat, in the opposite manner to 'normal' materials like metals. Stop complaining that this is all too hard to understand. Use it to explain why you left your condom where you did.

Do you really know the fax?

A SCOTSMAN FROM a remote croft in Caithness was performing experiments using cattle jawbones for hinges, heather for springs and metal plates buried in the ground as a source of electric current. Thereby, he invented the first electric clock. Then he moved to London and, on 27 May, 1843, patented a fax machine!

Alexander Bain invented the fax about 30 years before Alexander Bell invented the telephone. Bain set up his message in printer's type and then had a stylus wipe over it so as to make contact with the raised parts only. He moved it side to side with a pendulum, and incrementally downwards with a clockwork mechanism. Variable length dashes and spaces transmitted contact and non-contact.

At the receiving end, a similar stylus closed the circuit over a sheet of paper soaked in potassium ferrocyanide. The passing of electric current turned the paper black, thus reproducing the transmitted message.

The first commercial fax service opened in 1865 between Paris and Lyons. It involved writing a message on metal with an insulating ink then wrapping it around a cylinder, phonograph-style. The receiver was still the soggy, chemically soaked paper, wrapped around an identical machine. Caseli's Pantélégraphe was not a commercial success and died with the Franco-Prussian war in 1870. In 1878 the Telewriter (electrowriter) was adopted by the British Post Office but this worked by transmitting pen movements and could not send images off a sheet of paper. Telewriters were still in use until the 1960s.

Potassium ferrocyanide

In spite of its ominous name, potassium ferrocyanide is harmless and indeed used today as an anticaking agent for table salt. The salt label may declare its presence in modern nomenclature as potassium hexacyanoferrate (UK), or ancient as yellow prussiate of potash (USA), or just (E)536.

This was also the time when the original 'blue print' process was discovered. Potassium ferrocyanide mixed with a light-sensitive iron salt (ammonium ferric citrate) formed a blue pigment on exposure to sunlight. It was called Prussian blue or Turnbull's blue depending on the recipe for preparation, or patriotism.

The discovery in 1878 that elemental selenium changes its resistance and produces a current when exposed to light provided the first photographic exposure meters. (Mine still works—and it doesn't need batteries!) Light reflected from a black and white image onto a selenium plate thus provided an electric copy of the image.

This photoelectric effect was the basis of black and white xerography, invented in the United States in the 1930s. Xerography needed to be able to reproduce continuous tones and colour to make the invention useful and this was done by the South Australian Defence Standards Laboratory in 1953.

Selenium plates also provided a convenient erasable light sensitive plate for fax machines, and by 1920 newspapers were regularly sending photos down fax lines. The British meteorological office still uses these machines for transmission to regional stations which still print on Bain's original soggy electrolytic paper. No wonder the weather is so bad there!

Clever digital coding by an American mathematician, David Huffman, removed the enormous information redundancy inherent in any image and this speeded up transmission by orders of magnitude. The first digital fax, called the Dacom Rapidfax, was made in the United States in 1974.

The ubiquitous teleprinters used paper tape for their messages with six channels across the tape. The tape used an international code allowing a maximum of 56 characters. This was fine for Western alphabets, but useless for the 2000 or more characters needed for the Japanese script. So it was the Japanese who put in the resources to develop faxes commercially for themselves that were then cheap enough and fast enough to displace the teleprinter world-wide. The Japanese produced the circuitry for coding and the thermal printer using an American invention of a shiny waxy paper which goes black on heating (using a derivative of naphthalene—mothballs). It only needs the skill of putting a piece of paper with a message in the right way, dialling a number and pressing a button. That's my sort of technology.

Further Information

Tim Hunkin, 'Just give me the fax', *New Scientist*, 13 Februrary 1993 pp. 33–37; 'Invention and innovation', A. Walsh in *'From Stump-Jump Plough to Inter-scan: a review of invention and innovation in Australia*, pp. 23–4, Australian Academy of Science 1977.

Bonfires—is it safe to breathe outside?

'IN SOME PARTS of Lincolnshire they make fires in public streets, with bones of oxen, sheep, etc. heaped together', wrote a sixteenth-century scribe. The celebratory bone-fire of the Middle Ages has become our modern bonfire.

A burning log in winter, what bliss. The top part of the flame is bright yellow. The colour is caused by small particles of soot swept upwards and heated first red and then yellow hot. Less colour means cleaner burning. Near the base of the flame there is an area of faint blue where chemical reactions of free radicals produce light directly instead of heat. The embers are red hot and always seem to have exactly the same colour whether in the hotter middle or cooler edge of the fire.

Smoke results from incompletely combusted solids, and less benignly, we are today more aware of the volatile toxics that go with it. At least backyard rubbish burns are prohibited, if not personal ones called cigarettes. Burning a relatively low temperatures releases more carbon monoxide which combines with haemoglobin in our red blood cells about 250 times as strongly as does oxygen. Reduced oxygen in the blood is potentially lethal in those who already have a heart condition. The huge smog caused by fires in Indonesia in September 1997 caused illness in around 45 000 people and several deaths, and the Australian Government warned travellers with respiratory or heart problems to avoid the region for months (*Canberra Times*, 26 September 1997).

The smoke from incompletely combusted solids deposits in

the lungs. Red, streaming eyes and coughing from smoke are caused by breakdown gas products of cellulose, mainly acetic acid (vinegar) and propenal (acrolein). Wood smoke is around one-third as potent in causing mutations as car exhausts. It contains cancer-causing PAHs (polyaromatic hydrocarbons), dioxins and phosgene (a World War I war gas). No wonder smoke is considered too dangerous for use in smoked food; synthetic flavours are preferred!

And at the millennium and with the Olympics, just think of the pollution caused by fireworks displays! Fireworks owe their dazzle to heat, causing electrons to jump up inside metal atoms. When the electrons fall back, the pure colour characteristic for that metal is emitted, and indeed these colours are used for analysis. Sodium gives yellow, strontium red, and barium and copper give green.

But metals are not easily atomised at the lowly temperatures reached by burning gunpowder. In the form of metal chlorides, however, many will atomise. A kitchen experiment illustrates the effect. A piece of clean copper wire placed in a gas (stove) flame heats up but hardly adds colour to the flame. But touch a piece of PVC plastic with the hot wire so some melts and clings to the wire and reinsert it into the flame. It now turns the flame green. Insulated electric wire uses PVC plastic anyway, and you can do it all in one step.

And you guessed it. Modern fireworks mix in scrap powdered PVC, which is easy to formulate, but very polluting. The incomplete burning of the organic matter at a relatively low temperature in the presence of chlorine from PVC, along with metals to act as catalysts, provide the ideal conditions for the formation of dioxins, the most toxic of the pollutants from combustion. Sorry to be such a party pooper.

But now you are boned up about bonfires.

Hayfever—is it safe to breathe inside?

ACHOO. FOR ME, the hayfever season comes but once a year, with a vengeance. Others have it more often. Spring is the time when plants put their pollen into the wind and some of it winds up our sensitive noses.

Each grain of pollen carries on its surface a small amount of protein which is the 'signature' for its species. When the grain lands on a moist surface, the protein dissolves and is transferred to that surface. If it lands on a stigma waiting in the centre of another flower, the protein sends the message, 'Hey! I'm here, ready and waiting. Let's put it together.' This can lead to fertilisation and lots of potential baby plants. In our noses the message might be picked up by a grumpy immune system which lashes out at the unwelcome suitor with an attack of histamine. Attempts to treat the nose as a sex object are rejected with an attack of sneezing, eye watering or other unpleasant responses. Antihistamines are a great little earner for drug companies. Pharmacies look at fluff and pollen with glee. It will fill in the gap before the next winter flu.

Inside at home and in the office there are other problems. Many modern materials used indoors emit volatile organic chemicals (VOCs) which have adverse effects on workers breathing them in. They are also alleged to deposit subtle films on computer equipment which cause intermittent hardware failures.

Floor waxes are fast emitters, 90 per cent of the output all over in the first 30 minutes. In contrast, polyurethane lacquers are slower, taking 10 hours for a 90 per cent emission. Nitrogen oxides are emitted from unflued gas heaters. Photocopiers are notorious for the emission of ozone. Formaldehyde comes out of much modern furniture made from particle board and plywood. It is a potential carcinogen as well as an irritant.

Some products can absorb vapours and re-emit them slowly over time. Carpets, gypsum board and furnishings are in this category. Carpets are themselves major emitters of VOCs. The types and quantities depend on what the carpet and its associated materials are made of. Emissions from solvent-based adhesives, used in the glue down method, are a 100 to 1000 times higher than from the carpet itself. Carpet cushions, and 'seaming' compounds are also other significant sources. And then there are the fungi and mites.

Four common carpet types, two with styrene butadiene rubber (SBR) latex adhesive, one with a PVC (polyvinyl chloride) backing, the last with polyurethane backing, were tested and shown to emit different VOCs and at different concentrations.

In outdoor pollution, it is the products formed from reactions of VOCs (from fuel) and ozone that is the major concern. This outdoor process is catalysed by sunlight. But much the same products could be produced indoors as well; and with similar effects on us.

As well as sick offices, there are sick planes. Odours in aircraft are suspected of incapacitating cabin crews, and the British Aerospace BAe 146 plane is under suspicion. (See *Australian Financial Review*, 10 September 1999). About 35 are in operation in Australia alone. The culprit appears to be fumes from overheated oil leaking from the engines' hydraulic brakes, electrical components and even food heating facilities in the galleys.

Back to plants. They are not all of the nasty hay-fevering type. There are some goodies . . . A NASA scientist working on the problems of spacecraft air using a ground capsule called Biohome (Lunar 1 module) found a natural solution: indoor plants. In a book *How To Grow Fresh Air* (B.C. Wolverton, Penguin USA, 1997), the author listed what eats what. Azaleas, rubber plants, tulips, poinsettias and bamboo palms go for formaldehyde. For ammonia don't go past lady palm, and toluene is staple diet for areca palm. The peace lily is omnivorous and can take out acetone, methanol, ethanol, benzene, trichlorethylene and ethyl acetate. It will probably clean up emissions from your horrible after-shave or perfume as well.

This work was repeated in Australia. However, the reduction in pollutants was found to be neglibible (*New Scientist*, 15 January 2000). The effect was claimed to be psychological. Who cares? It's a great excuse to claim an allergy to the office.

OUT TO DINNER—
ALL FROTH AND BUBBLES

How stable is your foam?

STUDY A GLASS of beer with a magnifying glass. Just poured, the foam is thick and individual bubbles can adopt their natural spherical shape, some large, some small, but all happy, mobile and productive. Soon, however, the water drains out of the foam and the film of liquid becomes thinner. Individual bubbles are forced to amalgamate. They lose their round shape, and become polyhedrals, like in a honeycomb. The foam becomes coarser and eventually collapses. The beer is flat.

Does beer provide a warning of the consequences of globalisation?

They say you can float a 50 cent piece on the foam of a glass of Guinness. The fine cream foam in Guinness is stabilised with nitrogen gas, as well as carbon dioxide. Carbon dioxide, being quite soluble in water, diffuses quickly between bubbles and destabilises a foam. Air and nitrogen are much less soluble in water and therefore form more stable foams. When some of the grain used in making beer is replaced by other cheaper fermentables (like potatoes), the foam is reduced. Consumers interpret this as a loss of quality. So to rectify this perception, foam stabilisers called alginates made from seaweed extract are added. And the consumer is none the wiser. Not that there is anything wrong with seaweed! It breaks up on the beaches and foams the seawater.

The egg whites from which pavlovas are made make excellent foams, as a light delicate souffle, meringue (after the Swiss town of Meringen), Pavlova (ballet dancer), and angel cake attest. A pavlova foam needs to be beaten just right. This art is

Black Forest gateau

The best way to get cakes to dissolve rapidly on eating is to make them from foam. As we saw, the simplest kitchen foam is a meringue. The mousse for the base of the Black Forest cake is made from beating the whole egg and sugar. Industrial mousses are 'reinforced' with chalk dust, home kitchens use flour, but this has to be folded into the mixture to prevent starch particles from puncturing the bubbles. Fat is added to stop the starch crystallising out at room temperature, which will make the cake taste stale. But fat competes for the hydrophobic parts of the denatured protein, so the fat has to be folded in quickly and the cake placed in the oven as fast as possible. During baking, the proteins form stable cross-links and you get a solid cake instead of a gooey mess.

The cake expands about 10% in the oven, but once taken out, the steam condenses and the cake can collapse. To avoid this you should drop the cake (in the tin) onto a hard surface. This bursts some of the bubbles and allows some steam to escape before condensing. Well it's a great theory.

now understood by science. Egg whites consist mainly of a protein, albumen, in water. Left to their own devices, the molecules of this protein coil up with their hydrophobic parts inside. To get the coil to unwind, the protein has to have its internal bonds broken or 'denatured'. Whisking causes this breakdown and forces air into the mixture to form bubbles. The hydrophobic parts of the protein form a skin around the bubble and stabilise it.

The problem with any yolk in the mixture is the cholesterol which competes with the bubble air for the protein causing a drop in the volume of foam. When you are beating egg whites, plastic bowls, which tend to retain traces of fat, are to be avoided.

Sugar slows down the effect of beating. Sugar molecules also get in the way of protein molecules. When overbeating is a risk, like when you use an electric beater, adding sugar can be an advantage.

But, in contrast to fat, sugar enhances the stability of the foam in the oven by reducing drainage. This is because sugar molecules hold onto water molecules (through bonding to water's hydrogen atoms). You can beat without sugar, and then add it just before baking so as to have the best of both worlds of chemistry.

Early French cooking manuals in the 1770s are said to show the use of copper bowls in meringue making, a tradition that continues today. Recently, the chemical rationale for this was elucidated by the discovery that the protein in egg reacts with the tiny amount of copper dissolved from the bowl and this complex leads to even greater stability of the foam (see p. 80 on copper in the kitchen).

Where are bubbles born?

Wim BUBBLES, BE they soap bubbles, or an air bubble in a liquid or even a rubber balloon, the *smaller* the bubble, the *higher* the pressure inside the bubble. That is why it is so hard to start blowing up a balloon, but once started, blowing becomes easier. That is also why it is so hard for bubbles to start forming inside a liquid. They can't start of their own accord. For example, it is very difficult to form bubbles in water held in a clean smooth container. Heating water in such containers leads to 'bumping', whereby the water super-heats above 100°C and then leaves with a massive eruption. (Anti-bumping granules made from small porous pottery chips [with trapped air in crevices] are used to prevent bumping—but they do not work for airline bookings, ha ha). Bumping is a special danger in a microwave oven where the heating tends to be very uniform compared to a hotplate.

A closer look at bubbles

Does teaching science at dinner make eating out a tax deduction (or at least GST-free)?

An unshaken bottle of effervescent wine can be safely opened without a sudden rush of gas. Prolonged storage under pressure of 3 to 6 atmospheres pressure of carbon dioxide ensures that the internal glass surface has been thoroughly wetted and no sites are left for bubble formation. But as soon as the contents are poured into a clean dry glass, streams of bubbles will rise in the glass.

A wine waiter opens sparkling bottles by gently easing out the cork so that the gas trapped in the headspace is released over a prolonged time. This reduces the number of bubbles in the liquid that would act as 'crevices' for sudden release of dissolved gas. Conversely, deliberately adding bubbles to the sparkling wine, by shaking before opening, will increase gushing. Immediately after the stopper is removed, the waiter tilts the bottle over horizontally as far as possible, even to the extent of pouring some champagne into a glass. This minimises the expansion of bubbles coming up through the liquid and thereby takes more gas out of the sparkling. By reducing the vertical distance bubbles have to travel to reach the surface, the pressure drop, and thus expansion, is reduced.

Now we have the sparkling wine filled glass in front of us, and we examine it with a magnifying glass. The bubbles keep on coming from the *same* spots on the glass. These spots have small imperfections which trap tiny amounts of air.

A bubble forms when the carbon dioxide dissolved in the sparkling wine starts to move into the trapped air space, expanding it out of the crevice until it is buoyant enough to pinch off and float upwards. The gas moves into the crevice increasingly faster because a bigger bubble means *lower* pressure (remember the balloon) and so easier entry. As it floats away, expanding further as it rises, a new bubble starts to form in the same crevice.

Consumers allegedly prefer smaller, slow-moving bubbles in their effervescent wines, but such 'quality of the bead' criteria are a bit of an illusion, in spite of the criteria being included in the sensory analysis sheets for sparkling wines. 'Like all enduring totems, wine supports a diverse mythology, which is not confounded by its own contradictions.' (R. Barthes, 'Saponides et Détergents', 'Le Vin et Le lait' in *Mythologies*, Editions du Seuill, Paris, 1959.) Now for some close observation.

Each site emits bubbles of a uniform size and frequency, which can differ from site to site. The bubbles expand as they move up through the liquid, rapidly reaching a 'terminal' velocity as (anti-)gravity acceleration, that is, buoyancy, is opposed by the inertia and viscous drag of the liquid.

With time, the expansion on rising also decreases because there is less gas left to feed the bubbles in the surrounding liquid. Sparkling wines will therefore produce high frequency streams (10–20/sec) with little expansion during ascent because gas in the liquid above them has been depleted of dissolved carbon dioxide. As the gas content of the liquid is reduced, the number of emission sites decreases and also the bubbles' frequency (but not size) decreases. The distinctive appearance of effervescence in sparkling wines is mainly due to the presence of 10–12 per cent ethanol which lowers the surface energy and the solubility of carbon dioxide while raising the viscosity.

A transient collection of bubbles collects on the surface when sparkling wine is poured. This short-lived 'foam' is destroyed by the evaporation of the alcohol. It is more stable in a closed shaken bottle than in the poured glass. (You see the same effect comparing boiling liquids in covered saucepans to uncovered saucepans.)

Finally, surface active agents help stabilise foam and they are found in higher concentrations the 'closer' the product is to the natural biological origin. (You can show this by comparing the stability of foam by shaking closed containers of red and white, still and sparkling wines, beer, spirits, fruit juices, black tea, soft drinks, milk, and skim milk.)

Moving on, let us tackle the folklore that pouring beer or champagne into glasses from which the cleaning detergent has not been completely rinsed out, makes the drink go flat. Is that really so?

Well it is true that bubbling does drop dramatically after a short time in such a glass, but the drink starts off with the usual amount of gas, oblivious to the state of the glass into which it is about to be poured. The lack of bubbling suggests that the gas actually *stays in* the drink. Flatness is delayed rather than accelerated. Why is this so?

The detergent left on the glass surface would be expected to help wet this surface. In particular the small microcavities, which normally hold the trapped air that is the key to the formation and release of bubbles, will be filled with water instead of air, courtesy of the wetting properties of the detergent. The drink thus has less air-filled crevices to release bubbles. You can confirm this by adding a convenient bubble source such as sugar cubes to the drink. Sugar cubes contain lots of trapped air and are therefore an excellent source of bubbles. The alleged 'flat' drink will suddenly release a rush of bubbles.

In effervescent drinks without alcohol, the bubbles tend to be larger before detachment (the surface energy is higher, ~70 Nm^{-1} for water compared to ~50 Nm^{-1} with 10 per cent alcohol added), the speed of rising is faster (lower viscosity), and the larger bubbles tend to flatten and wobble during their ascent.

In plastic bottles (PET and others), there is a strong attraction between the bottle wall and the bubble, which, compared to glass bottles, has to be much larger before detaching. In a plastic container of aerated water, the bubbles can become quite large and yet remain attached to the side as they rise. The reason is that both bubbles and plastic are hydrophobic (repel water), whereas clean glass is hydrophilic (water-attracting). Thus bubbles would rather cling to the plastic wall than be released into that unloved water. The same happens inside plastic straws.

As the meal comes to a close, it is time for some liqueurs such as port, brandy or Cointreau. When poured, a thin film will rise on a ring around the inside of the glass above the liquid surface due to the surface energy of the liquid. Its height depends on the cleanliness of the glass and the alcohol content of the liquid. It is a few millimetres high for wine but can be a hefty ten millimetres for a proof liqueur (it drops again for drinks of much higher alcohol levels). As alcohol evaporates from this film, the surface energy rises and the film thickens at the top and forms droplets. As these become bigger and heavier they slip down the side to meet the surface of the bulk liquid in the glass. However, they have trouble re-entering the bulk because their loss of alcohol and consequent higher surface energy oppose mixing, and a sort of kissing of the surface by the drop often occurs whereby the drop actually extracts liquid from the bulk before eventually succumbing to envelopment. These tears on wine or legs on port are a fitting study for a meal's end.

Soon fresh aromatic coffee will be served. A bubbly sound now assails the ear—the merry singing of the kettle. The singing comes from bubbles of steam formed near the hot element where the water is super-heated. That is, it is heated above the normal boiling point of water ($100^{0}C$ at sea level). The super-heated steam bubble rises into the cooler water above. There it suddenly collapses into oblivion by dissolving in the water, at the same time sending out a supersonic shock wave.

This process happens cyclically, like a loudspeaker feeding into a mike, and gives a similar singing effect. As the water in the kettle becomes hotter, the bubbles rise further before collapsing, and the pitch drops. Just before the kettle boils, the bubbles reach the surface and the singing stops completely.

And so must I.

SERIOUS STUFF

Speciation and oxidation number

WE TEND TO stereotype cultures, nations and people because classifying makes it easier to organise our feelings and responses. Meet someone—she reminds us of someone else. Bang! She goes into a preselected slot unless or until otherwise revealed. Chemicals are dealt with in much the same way. Chemists are more careful in their judgements than the lay person but we all tend to jump to conclusions.

We say things like, 'Chromium is carcinogenic', but the expert understands this in a much more circumscribed way. Before labelling a chemical with certain properties it is crucial to define exactly to what degree the chemical has 'access' to the organism—how available it is biologically.

Let us start with an analogy: wealth. Assets come in a variety of forms which differ in their degree of ready availability. They range from cash, cheque and debit accounts, credit cards, listed shares, unlisted instruments, real estate, other property and so on. 'What are you worth?' is thus not an easy question to answer off the top of your head.

'How much of this chemical will make me sick?' isn't easy to answer either. I've been asked at a party, 'How much arsenic is in this lobster?' Well, actually it's a helluva lot. Some crustaceans contain up to 100 milligrams per kilogram (dry weight) of arsenobetaine, hundreds of times over the Australian legal food limits for 'ordinary' arsenic. However, the arsenic is not present in its usual form, as found in natural ores, old sheep dip formulations, or weed killer, but is attached to other elements that hang onto it so strongly that it passes through our gut unchanged. Thus, it isn't a problem if it isn't 'available' to the body to do damage.

How much aluminium is in the water supply? In the form of clay it doesn't matter. In the dissolved form we can absorb (coming out of the concrete pipes on its way to our taps), there should be concern.

Chemicals are thus like money. In some forms and situations they are easily accessed, while in others they are not.

Sometimes copper comes out of water pipes and gives you blue rings on the bathtub, diarrhoea and kills the goldfish. This can happen when pipes are new, before the protective insoluble crust has formed on the pipe's surface. Copper does not leach (is not available) from older pipes.

As we saw earlier, the tangy taste of tomato soup is by courtesy of the tin dissolved from the inside of the can rather than the tomato. Unlike cans for other foods, tomato soup ones are generally only partially lacquered to allow this to happen. Tin is deliberately made available. Too much tin tastes metallic but there is no health issue.

In spite of what Popeye used to tell us, iron in spinach is not readily available to the body while iron in meat is. Iron occurs in a different chemical form in these two foods. Farmers spread superphosphate regularly because it soon loses its availability as the soil locks the phosphorus up again. The party is over and flies gather on the scraps. A zap of spray containing pyrethroids quickly zonks them. It drifts into the fish pond and zonks the fish as well—unless the water is muddy because clay absorbs this chemical and locks it up like superphosphate, only faster.

Chemists call these different forms in which the same species can appear *speciation*. For nitrogen we speak of the gas dinitrogen in the air, nitrous oxide (laughing gas) as an anaesthetic, nitrites in food, nitrates in ground water and ammonia in the laundry.

One attempt to help close in on the speciation of the element in a particular situation is to define for it an *oxidation state*. This is a method that avoids things you just don't want to hear about, like outer electron shells, valence, and balancing chemical equations! But for those who just have to know . . . the oxidation state of an element in a covalent bond is the charge it would possess if the shared electrons were transferred completely to the more electron-grabbing (electronegative) atom(s), giving the latter their filled rare-gas shell. It is an accounting scheme only vaguely related to chemical theory. Like all accounting schemes, its rules are (somewhat) arbitrary.

Good old water is given the formula H_2O because in water two hydrogen atoms link to one oxygen atom. Now, we assign the charge +1 to an atom of hydrogen and a charge of –2 to an atom of oxygen. Adding these 'assignments' up for H_2O gives 2 x (+1) plus 1 x (–2) = 0. This is consistent because a water molecule is neutral, that is, it has no charge.

When O and/or H are attached to other atoms, like nitrogen, sulfur and carbon, we can calculate their oxidation numbers depending on the circumstances in which these atoms find themselves in a particular molecule.

Take ammonia, NH_3, for instance. The atom of nitrogen, attached as it is to three hydrogens, must get the number –3, because ammonia is also a neutral molecule. When attached to oxygen, as in laughing gas, N_2O, nitrogen must be +1. For nitric oxide, NO, nitrogen must be +2. And in nitrogen dioxide, NO_2, nitrogen must be +4.

Unlike water, which is neutral, with nitrites there is a charge of minus one, thus creating an ion. The nitrite ion is $(NO_2)^-$ (called N, O, two, minus). So nitrogen here must be +3 to allow for the negative charge. The nitrate ion is $(NO_3)^-$ (called N, O, three, minus). Here nitrogen becomes +5, again allowing for the negative charge. For nitrogen gas, N_2, with two identical nitrogens attached to each other to form a neutral molecule, each is assigned the number zero.

Molecules in which atoms show their more positive (or less negative) values are called oxidised or higher oxidation states. With lower or more negative values, they are called reduced, reducing or lower oxidation states. Nitrogen moves down the scale from nitrate (+5), nitrite (+3), nitric oxide (+2), nitrogen (0), to ammonia (–3). (There are also molecules where nitrogen finds itself with the missing numbers of –1 and –2.)

Sulfur, S, ranges as well. In rotten egg gas, H_2S, or mineral sulfides, it sits at –2. In elemental sulfur, S, it is zero. In sulfur dioxide, SO_2, or in sulfite ion $(SO_3)^{2-}$, sulfur is +4. For sulfur trioxide, SO_3, or in sulfate ion $(SO_4)^{2-}$, sulfur is +6.

The same can be done for carbon. Thus methane, CH_4, puts

carbon at –4; carbon monoxide, CO, places it at +2; while for carbon dioxide, CO_2, it must be +4.

So why is this chemical abacus interesting?

Out in the swamp, in putrescent compost, and in landfill where air is excluded, these elements will always be in their reduced forms (lower numbers). Nitrogen will be bound as ammonia and nitrite. (It's also nitrite in air-excluded preserved canned meat.) Carbon will be found as methane and sulfur as rotten egg gas, or sulfide (often called potential acid sulfate soil). Exposed to the air by excavation or agriculture, the more oxidised forms (higher oxidation states) prevail; nitrogen as nitrate; sulfide soil converted to sulfate and then released as sulfuric acid into the environment.

For carbon, the lower the oxidation state, the better the material is a a fuel, because in raising it up the number scale (by burning), a great deal of energy is released. We burn methane (C = –4) from landfill gas, or natural gas; or we burn carbon (as coal or coke, C = 0); in both cases we produce carbon dioxide (C = +4). So we push carbon from –4 (or 0) to +4. Butane, C_4H_{10}, is a typical component of petrol. Here carbon is –2.5, not as good as methane (–4) but better than coal (0).

What about when we use oxygenated fuel such as alcohol C_2H_5OH so as to lower pollution? Well, the same rules can be applied. Carbon in alcohol scores –2. Alcohol is a somewhat poorer fuel than butane because it already has some oxygen included in its molecule. As oxygen contributes –2 to the sum, the carbon must contribute a more positive value to the total, going from –2.5 in butane to –2 in alcohol.

If the low numbers constitute fuel, what about the high numbers? Well, these can supply the oxygen for burning. Nitrates are used in gunpowder. Ammonium nitrate is a fertiliser but also, when mixed with diesel fuel, an explosive.

Hydrazine, N_2H_4, and hydrogen peroxide, H_2O_2, are both used in rocket fuels. In hydrazine, nitrogen takes the missing –2 value (from our scheme for nitrogen earlier). In hydrogen peroxide, oxygen is now assigned –1 instead of the usual –2, keeping hydrogen fixed. On rare occasions even the value of hydrogen must be changed—remembering the numbers are set by the rule of assigning electrons to the most electron-grabbing atom(s) and this can be ambiguous at times.

There was a single reaction that made me determined to

become a chemist. That concerned nitrogen triodide, NI_3, which can be made from household chemicals. If a tiny amount is pasted wet on a blackboard duster or smeared on the floor and let dry, it will detonate at the touch of a fly (or teacher).

We saw that N in ammonia was –3. When elemental iodine is added (oxidation state zero) to ammonia (N oxidation state –3) it forms NI_3, plus 3HI. Iodine is now iodide in this compound and moves down to oxidation state –1. Nitrogen moves up to +3. For the cognoscenti, a change for one nitrogen from –3 to +3 (or six iodines, each from 0 to –1), means six electrons have been transferred to balance the books, $3I_2 + NH_3 \rightarrow NI_3 + 3HI$. (Incidentally, chemical bookkeepers use Roman numerals in these accounts. But then they use Latin and Greek numerical prefixes in their formulas for specific meanings. All very alchemical . . .)

Back to the beginning. Chrome plate is quite safe. It is chromium at +6, written as Cr^{VI}, that is dangerous and thus not used much these days. What about mercury—it's a toxic heavy metal? What is that mouthful of mercury amalgam doing to us (oldies)? Liquid mercury was once used to cure constipation as it just pushed its way through the bowels. Elemental liquid mercury is not poisonous in that form (0), although the mechanical effects in the bowel can be disastrous. As an inhaled vapour, mercury (still 0) is poisonous, and fresh amalgams do release some vapour. The older ones quickly become oxidised and inert. Mercury (I) tends to be found in insoluble compounds and tends therefore not to be very harmful. But mercury (II) compounds can be soluble and very poisonous. Mercury attached to organic groups is extremely toxic because it dissolves in body fats.

Crucial chemical and biochemical processes depend on the changing oxidation states of certain elements. These range from photosynthesis converting sunlight to food and fuel, the biochemical energy providers in our bodies [ATP/ADP], and winning metals from ores which is the reverse process of corrosion. The chemical abacus allows us to balance these chemical energy books, but like all accountancy, it often fails to be transparent to the outsider.

Borrowed time

WE ARE TOLD that in Heaven and on Earth there is continuous conflict between good and evil, God and Satan. In chemistry, Time and Temperature battle it out for revealing the Path to be trodden. Well, not quite 'temperature', but it sounds better and is more familiar than 'equilibrium thermodynamics'. And not quite 'time' either . . . kinetics is the term used.

How far and how fast? These are the eternal chemical questions. A modern chemist Hamlet ponders life on this mortal coil, of products made from iron, steel and plastic; the sensitivity of computer chips to radiation in space; and the stability of the chemicals that form our genes.

Thermo (to its friends) calculates the ultimate fate of a chemical process. How far will it go before stopping? Iron and steel rust; plastic disintegrates; computer chips fail; and genes mutate. Salt and water will spontaneously mix but never unmix on their own. (See p. 103 on osmosis).

Kinetics, a stand-in for time, guestimates how fast things will go. How much will painting slow down rust, or shielding protect chips? Kinetics is a far less exact science (and has fewer friends). But tarted up in recent years as Irreversible Thermo, it has won the odd Nobel prize.

Is petrol stable? Not a psychological but a chemical question. It can hang around in the tank for yonks but a flash in the pan can give rise to an unholy explosion (see p. 54, on reaching flashpoint). Very little incentive transforms petrol or natural gas into water vapour, carbon dioxide and a helluva lot of energy. And there is no simple way to reverse this process and put the genie back into the bottle. Sure, you can absorb the water and carbon dioxide by growing a crop of trees for a few decades. Then you can chop them down and bury them in a swamp for few millennia to form some peat. But, oh, how slow. This is not a real answer to the greenhouse effect.

Our bodies are chemically unstable as well. Something as inherently complex and hence unlikely as a human being needs a great deal of ingenious continuous internal chemistry to survive against the forces of decay decreed by Thermo.

The good fight is fought with converted solar energy (in the form of food) to rebuild our tissues and keep at bay bacteria that attempt to use us for food for themselves. Enzymes run exquisite chemical factories inside every cell of our bodies, each with its own task and time scale. All is far from equilibrium and most processes do not get a chance to go on and complete their theoretical paths before another takes over and moves matters in yet another direction. Cycles are linked together in multi-dimensional chemical relay races, never starting, never ending. Until death and decay do us part. Then the worms and bacteria use us as part of their cycles.

Hard and soft in chemistry

I AM AN analogue person. While admiring the ever better calculations available from ever more powerful computers, I can't help feeling that a quite precise answer from a complex model whose inner assumptions are known only to some distant programmer leaves one intellectually vulnerable. A rough answer from a simple comprehensible model is insightful and satisfying.

It's a fact. Chemical elements chose some partners with whom they like to be combined in preference to others. The theoretical justification of this chemical observation followed a long and painful path. Early important contributions were seen in the 1940s. These advanced in the 1950s, and some aspects were publicised in the 1960s by double Nobel laureate Linus Pauling (chemistry and peace). The 'hard' and 'soft' concept was suggested by R.G. Pearson in 1963 ('Hard and Soft Acids and Bases', *Journal of the American Chemists' Society*, vol. 85, pp. 35339).

Computers since the 1980s have refined our calculations on chemical bonds *ad nauseum* but in doing so have lost the essential simplicity and overview that analogue models provide. Revisiting the 1960s, one can rediscover an innocence and grandeur of approach that in many ways provides a superior way of chemical thinking, certainly for learning.

Silver metal is bright and shiny. Silvery actually. It sits around in clean air and is unaffected by oxygen. However, a whiff of sulfur, either in the air (from burnt fuels) or in a trace of protein in the sweat of the fingers or white of an egg, and

Road digs

Interestingly, in the gold-mining town of Kalgoorlie in Western Australia, mine waste was used for road building until it was realised that the waste contained significant quantities of a natural black gold compound, gold telluride. Gold had chosen tellurium, the relatively rare big, big brother of sulfur, as its sole chemical partner in nature. And it did it enough to make the locals dig up the roads again to extract it.

the silver turns black. Silver sulfide has formed. Black silver sulfide is the bane of the host of the formal dinner party.

If silver tarnishes, why not gold? Gold is almost always found as the free metal which made it an object of value to the earliest of societies. Well gold *does* react with sulfur just like silver, but it forms a single layer of tarnish invisible to the eye which protects it from further attack. The layer of sulfur on gold is actually very difficult to remove. It is held so tenaciously that it needs to be roasted off.

There is a tradition of painting liquid gold on porcelain and firing the decorated piece. How was the liquid gold prepared? The artists used vegetable oils treated with sulfur which acted as a solvent for gold. So gold and sulfur are preferred partners again.

The old masters used a lot of lead pigment in the paint of their pictures—white basic lead carbonate where lead is attached unwillingly to oxygen (see later). Over the centuries, this has tarnished to black due to the formation of lead sulfide. Lead is back to its preference for sulfur over oxygen. (But an overdose of oxygen in the form of hydrogen peroxide can restore old masters—as well as their pseudo-blonde mistresses—but not to the original pigment. The white regained is lead sulfate not carbonate.) In nature lead is found mainly as a sulfide ore called galena.

Copper, on the other hand, when left outside attaches itself to oxygen. It forms an attractive green patina which is a mish-mash of oxide, hydroxide and carbonate. Copper couldn't care less about sulfur unless there is no air around. Copper ores tend to be carbonate-related.

When the earth formed it was bit like a modern steel blast-furnace. Molten metals mixed and sank to the bottom (centre of the earth) and a slag floated to the top. Weathering then mucked the slag around a bit. (Geology for beginners!!.) It is in that 'slag' that we find our minerals.

Certain metals which liked sulfur ended up as sulfide ores while others which liked touching oxygen are found as oxides, carbonates, silicates and sulfates.

The old but elegant theory goes something like this. If the atom is large then its outer electrons (or holes) can be easily pushed around (the electrons are said to polarisable) and the label 'soft' is given to it. It helps if there aren't too many electrons (or holes) in the outside orbits. If the atom is small then the pushing around of outer electrons is more difficult (the electrons are said to be non-polarisable). The label 'hard' is given. It helps if there are several electrons (or holes) in the outside orbits. Simply (or simplistically), hard reacts with hard and forms polar bonds. The atoms swap electrons and take on plus and minus charges. The resulting compound is often water-soluble. Soft reacts with soft and forms non-polar bonds. The positive and negative charges are only separated a short distance. The resulting compound is often water-insoluble.

Hard

Most of the common light (near the top of the Periodic Table of the elements) metals, like sodium, calcium, magnesium, aluminium and titanium, are hard. Non-metals, like oxygen and fluorine, are hard. And in saying oxygen, we include groups in which oxygen is the atom that touches the metal, like sulfate, carbonate, silicate, acetate and other organics. It is the oxygen atom that is actually doing the hand-holding with the metal.

Soft

Many heavy (near the bottom of the Periodic Table of the elements) metals, like silver, lead, mercury and gold, are soft. Non-metals, like carbon, phosphorus, sulfur, bromine and iodine, are soft. And the electron on its own is considered to be the ultimate in softness.

Borderline

The metals iron, cobalt, nickel and copper are borderline. Iron (III), stripped of its outer electrons is hard, but leaving one electron behind to form Fe(II) keeps it a little soft. The non-metals nitrogen and chlorine are borderline.

So in nature you tend to find sodium and calcium carbonates (but not sulfides) because light metals like oxygen, and silver and lead sulfides (but not carbonates) because heavy metals like sulfur. All can form chlorides. You find iron(II) sulfide but iron(III) oxide. (The oxidation of the former of these to the latter when exposed to air is the cause of the environmental disaster that goes by the name acid soil formation. As the rules suggest, when iron loses an outer electron, it moves from soft to hard and shifts its attraction from sulfur to oxygen.)

Health and toxicity

The ions of all soft (heavy) metals are toxic at quite low levels. Mercury, lead, cadmium and thallium are the classic examples. The reason that they are toxic is as follows. When ingested as soluble compounds, these heavy metals react readily with the sulfur atoms in the proteins of our bodies that form bridges that give the protein its three-dimensional structure. That structure allows the protein to carry out its essential metabolic functions. On contact with the metal, the bridge is broken and the structure is destroyed.

The heavy metal–sulfur bond represents a typical soft-soft embrace. The metal–sulfur compound formed tends to be insoluble in water and thus not easily excreted. It is stored in the fatty tissues instead.

The chemicals used as hair colour restorers tend to be heavy metal compounds (see p. 137). Lead acetate is a common active component (at around half a per cent). The lead is attached to oxygen in the acetate and is happy to exchange that for an attachment to sulfur in the growing hair protein (keratin) to produce black lead sulfide in a grey hair. Just don't lick your fingers after massaging the lotion into the scalp.

And why do gold miners use cyanide to extract gold metal from crushed ore? Well, cyanide is a real softie and as the rule predicts, reacts readily with (heavy) metal softies, including gold.

The use of cyanide to lure gold out of its ore has its downsides. The drinking water of 2.5 million Hungarians has been poisoned with cyanide and fish killed by a spill from an Australian joint venture mine in Romania. A not uncommon tragedy accompanying this soft-soft love affair.

Long and short—
Fourier transforms

IDEAS IN QUANTUM mechanics have revolutionised twentieth-century understanding of the behaviour of the fundamental particles of which matter is composed: atoms, electrons, light and much else. It is a theory that is expounded in the language of mathematics in which few are fluent and this makes it pretty inaccessible. But language makes wide use of metaphor, analogy and allegory. Amazingly, music can be used to tell stories without words and it is via music that I want to tell some of the stories of the quantum world.

The orchestra is warming up before a performance. The audience hushes as the the piano and violin each play a single note; the violinist adjusts the tension in the string looking for a common pitch with the piano. Each instrument is playing the note at a slightly different pitch. What you hear as a result is a beating. You appear to be hearing a single pitch that varies periodically in loudness. As the violin adjusts closer to the piano, the frequency with which the loudness varies (the beat frequency) slows down until it finally doesn't vary at all any more, and the two instruments are now 'in tune'.

You shut your eyes enthralled by this simple, wonderful activity. But what is the reality? Two notes of different pitch played at the same time or one pitch fluctuating rythmically in loudness? Turn the violin off and you hear the single note of the piano. No beats. The same if you reverse the choice. What you hear one at a time is not what you hear together. Should you believe the logic of a single addition or the perception of that addition? The answer is surprisingly easy. Both. Both interpretations are correct and at the same time.

Sound moves through the air in waves, and one of the properties of waves is that they can interfere, that is, they can cancel each other out or reinforce each other in time or in space (see pp. 90–2).

Light going through a small hole in a screen forms a single spot on a cardboard screen behind. Light going through another small hole shifted ever so slightly from the first does the same but, naturally, shifted ever so slightly on the screen. Light going through both slits at the same time forms a complex 'beat pattern' of spots on the screen. Light waves can thus show interference in space, which is what sound waves show in time.

Physicists decided that it was useful to think of particles behaving as waves. They applied this to electrons, atoms and even big things, although the effect is then too small to be measured. This allows them to make analogies with other waves, like sound and light.

Outside it is dark and there is one street light visible through a curtain. The curtain is woven from yarns interlaced in two dimensions, warp across the weft, to form a grid of fibres. This mini-grid does in two dimensions what the two holes with light pouring through did in one dimension: cause interference of the light waves and a pattern of single spots in different places of different brightness surrounding the central spot from the street light. (A laser pointer shining through some curtain material gives a sharper effect.)

The orchestra starts to play and all the instruments furiously produce notes. With so many instruments the music is far too complex for most mortals to analyse. Just enjoy the composer's genius.

Too complex to analyse was also the problem faced by Rosalind Franklin working meticulously in her laboratory in Cambridge. She, too, was shining a beam of light at a 'cloth' and analysing the patterns formed. In her case the 'cloth' was a speck of DNA with the bonded atoms forming the weft and warp. The atomic pattern is so small, however, that ordinary light waves are too long to show interference, but X-ray waves are of perfect pitch. The pattern of spots formed by the DNA exposed to a beam of X-rays was caught on an X-ray film which she then developed. Every one of the many thousands of spots needed to be catalogued, meticulously recording its position and brightness (darkness of the spot on the film). The task was then to work backwards from the catalogued spots to the structure of the DNA molecule that gave rise to them. This is analogous to working out the cloth pattern from the pattern of spots made by the laser beam shone through the cloth. It is difficult because information is lost in the diffraction process as spots cannot be of negative intensity, at worst zero. Waves, on the other hand, can have both positive and negative amplitude. This loss of information is called the phase problem. The early computers available for these analyses had difficulty coping with this problem unless given some hint as to what the correct answer might be. Looking over her shoulder, Watson and Crick were inspired to make the right guess and reap the rewards of a Nobel prize.

Until recently, mainly women did this work called X-ray crystallography. Women did all the boring, hard slog bits of the research, as they are still doing in molecular biology laboratories today. Things change only slowly.

The orchestra has become silent allowing one lone flautist to play a long, lingering pure note. If she plays a short note, it will be less pure. Making it shorter still produces a nasty squawk with no recognisable pitch. Short is not sweet. You cannot have a pure tone which is also short.

The implications of this observation range across the deepest meanings in quantum mechanics, through measuring coastlines, to the push for digital television. Why is that so?

For a note to be short it has to start from nothing, quickly build up to something, and decay quickly to nothing again. That's the meaning of short. A single pitch (sound) has a (sine) wave that goes on forever, no start, no finish. The only way to make a short 'packet' of sound is to add together lots of sine waves with different frequencies (pitches/harmonics/overtones) so that they 'cancel out' at both ends. The diagram shows how adding progressively more frequencies (shown as vertical bars plotted horizontally) can give you a shorter wave packet in space (or time).

Returning to the quantum mechanic's view of the micro world, everything (light, photons, radio waves, atoms, electrons and other subatomic particles) is visualised as something like these packets of waves. A packet tends to be called a wave when

Sound waving

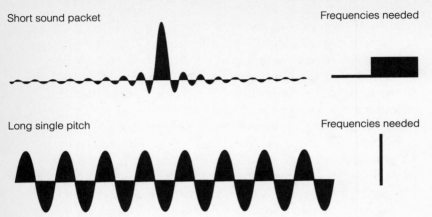

Short sound packet

Frequencies needed

Long single pitch

Frequencies needed

spread out, but called a particle when it is more localised. This is sometimes called the particle–wave paradox. All a bit uncertain.

Now here comes the rub. It is the frequencies of waves that are related to almost everything you want to know, like energy, speed, momentum. Want certainty about these attributes? Then you can only have few frequencies. Aha, that means a spread-out wave, and uncertainty as to where 'it' is. A pure note (few frequencies) means a long note in time (or space).

Heisenberg based his famous uncertainty principle on a brilliant mathematical relationship for wave packets discovered by Jean Baptiste Joseph Fourier. Fourier had been sentenced to the guillotine by Robespierre during the French terror of 1794. Luckily the execution was due the day following the tyrant's overthrow, so with his mind much concentrated, he gave us the famous Fourier Transform with its enormous applications. These range over data enhancement of photographs from space, chemical analysis and forensic examination of sound (Watergate) tapes. Our ears, eyes and brains also appear to interpret sensual stimulus with this transform process.

Using a set of ever increasing higher frequency component waves of the same (sinusoidal) shape means that Fourier analysis is fractal. For example, you can get a crude outline of the Australian coast by tracing a fairly smooth line around to form a certain shape. To define major inlets you add a curve that goes in and out more often, that is, a higher frequency. The more components of higher frequency, the better the fit (and the longer the coastline).

Fourier analysis also answers the following question: If TV and radio stations are each allocated a single, discrete frequency at which to transmit, why can't we have as many stations as we like in an allocated band? As long as no information is transmitted, you can.

Transmitting any sort of information (sound or picture) immediately shortens the waves and converts the single, sharp carrier to a band of frequencies. With analogue transmission this widening is quite substantial (more for FM than AM). Digital is smarter. But just chopping a single pure frequency into short digital bits automatically spreads it to many frequencies, just like the flautist shortening her note made it lose its pure tone and become a mixture of many pitches. That's the long and short of it.

I do wonder whether Heisenberg played the flute.

Reference

Ben Selinger, *MacFourier 2.6*, Oxford University Press, Oxford, 1991.

Empathy with entropy

IT IS NO coincidence that Dr Who was addicted to jelly beans. They can reveal a lot about the universe.

Take 400 white jelly beans (or better still, spherical sweets like Jaffas) and place them on a tray roped off just enough to hold them loosely. Then add 50 red ones in a group together. Now use your fingers to mix the beans up randomly. The group of red beans will spread amongst the white and will never 'unspread' again.

But is it random? You'll see red clusters of two, and three, and so on. What really is random?

You could also start by placing the red ones singly (uniformly) amongst the white ones so all the reds are isolated from each other by white. The reds are all in a 'cluster of one', so to speak.

Mixing will again give roughly the same selection of clusters of two and three as before. You find a few clusters of four or five. A few more of three, more still of two and lots of one. But clusters of 'none' are the most common. Yeah, it's a bit of a fiddle to decide when it is a cluster, and you can move the boundaries if you want, gerrymander the electorates, so to speak, but in the end it really makes no difference.

The bottom line is that the *number* of clusters through the sizes zero, one, two, three, or four, et cetera, falls off roughly exponentially and is the same (within sampling error) with every mixing. It is only *where* the clusters turn up, that changes with each new mix.

That's a pretty fishy result and in fact it was a French mathematician called Poisson whose maths explained all. What starts off spread around in uniform small packets and is allowed to randomise always ends up clustering in this most peculiar manner.

Punters go to a casino, all with say roughly the same money to stake. They come out with winnings exponentially distributed. Most with nothing. More with some. Few with a big win.

Other punters buy insurance with roughly the same premium. At the end of the year, most have done their dough. A modest number have had modest claims met, and a few have needed big payouts. An organisation (society) might start with everybody equal. But it quickly changes to a hierarchy. A few people have a lot of influence, many have some, most have none.

Incomes distribute themselves likewise; it is the aim of a progressive tax system to try and reverse this 'natural' tendency, but with little success. Even when we control the events, like organising a lottery, we would never arrange it so all the prizes were exactly the same modest value, with no chance of a big one. It just wouldn't seem 'natural'.

Illnesses can tend to cluster in time or space 'naturally' and epidemiologists have the Devil's own trouble sorting out whether there is an overriding medical cause for the cluster. Cars bunch up along a road (even without traffic lights) giving you a chance to cross at some stage. Birthdays bunch up, too. So much so that in a group as small as 23, there is a fifty-fifty chance that two people will have their birthdays on the same day.

Because this cluster distribution is so pervasive, any absence of a particular-sized cluster gets people looking for it. If the pattern of different-sized oil wells in a geographic area doesn't conform, then it suggests that it might be worth looking for the missing size(s). The sizes of cities in a country, grants for research, number of letters in a word, frequency of the letters of the alphabet in a piece of text (of great importance to code-breakers), all follow this amazing pattern.

Deep physical consequences arise because all the particles, molecules and materials from which the universe is constructed are driven by this non-reversible effect of mixing, as summarised in the second law of the thermodynamics (which says, in its simplest form, that entropy—overall—always increases).

So next time you play the pokies, why not chew a jelly bean, grit your teeth and think of entropy. (A more detailed explanation of this with maths and computer modelling is given in my *Chemistry in the Marketplace*, Allen & Unwin, 1998.)

Radioactivity revisited

MY BRAIN IS addled as I try to write. It is cold. My computer screen gets a severe case of the wobbles. Why is that so?

The in-slab electric heating is automatically switched on by the off-peak power supply. The heater coil winds through the floor slab and acts as an aerial. A magnetic field of the order of 50 to 70 milligauss (mG) is passing through the monitor (and me) 50 times per second. I know what it does to the monitor (10–15 mG will start to annoy it). What does it do to me?

Because of concerns about electromagnetic emissions from high voltage power lines and the like, the *National Health and Medical Research Council* in 1989 set a recommended limit for continuous 24-hour exposure of no more than 1000 mG. Fine, however. . . 'There remains some controversy with the issue because epidemiological studies sometimes show elevated health risk at much lower values', Colin Roy, Head of the NIR section in the Commonwealth Department of Health and Aged Care, informs us.

Hmmm.

NIR stands for non-ionising radiation. This refers to alternating electric current, radio waves and microwaves (including those of mobile phones). The effects of NIR are more subtle than those from ionising radiation but probably cause no more than poor writing style!

In stark contrast, the alpha, beta and gamma rays emitted by radioactive material are powerful enough to knock electrons off atoms and turn atoms into ions. This makes them very reactive.

The world's car tyres and condoms are irradiated to cross-link the rubber molecules and give the product strength. Irradiation is useful for killing bugs. Bulk pharmaceuticals can be sterilised dry by irradiation but in solution they lose their potency. The classic case is insulin where irradiation in solution causes a subtle geometry change in an amino acid, o-tyrosine, to a form not found in nature, and this causes loss of drug activity. This change in geometry is now used as an indicator of irradiation of any product in solution that contains protein.

Tampons are sterilised with irradiation. At one time when local stocks had run out, a product was imported from New Zealand which had been sterilised conventionally with the chemical ethylene oxide. This batch of tampons was non-sterile and caused the outbreak of toxic shock in Australia. I wonder how safe advertised organic tampons are!

The Australian and New Zealand Food Authority (ANZFA) recently legalised food irradiation in Australia and a facility is planned for Queensland to treat tropical fruit. Irradiated food is not radioactive but changes do occur, as indeed they do with conventional preservatives and cooking.

Japanese studies show that water-soluble vitamins are destroyed by heavy irradiation and the destruction is proportional to the water content, just as for pharmaceutical products. Thus wheat (7% water) and spices are unaffected. Potatoes must be irradiated at just the right time to stop sprouting and avoid skin damage. If not, they will turn black.

From years on the Council of the Australian Consumers Association, I know that consumers are mainly concerned that irradiation might be used to allow food hygiene standards to be relaxed. The United States has had several fatal episodes of bacterial-contaminated hamburgers but has facilities to irradiate only about 5 per cent of the beef consumed. This does raise anxiety about the safety of the other 95 per cent!

One of the major uses of irradiation is on prawns from South-East Asia, where high rates of infection in aquafarming are common. However, irradiation causes the heads to fall off! Beware the headless prawn cutlet!

Back in mid-1973 chest X-rays for TB (carried out from mobile units) were still compulsory. I accidentally wore my radiation monitor on my belt for one of these. When my monitor was routinely read panic broke out. It said that I had been exposed to over five years' worth of occupational radiation!

Fatal meat

One hundred million hamburgers were withdrawn from the US market on 23 August 1997—one for every adult in the nation. It was the largest food recall in US history. About 11 million kilograms of beef were withdrawn by the Hudson Food Company as it indefinitely closed its plant in Columbia, Nebraska—because of an E.coli scare. Sixteen people had died in Colorado the month before.

Hudson practice was to refrigerate unused meat at the end of the day and mix it with new chilled (but not fresh) meat the next day. When a batch of contaminated meat was traced back to the company, it had by that time infected the meat in the intervening days. All the meat had to be recalled. Industry wants to introduce irradiation. But there will never be enough units and improving handling and hygiene is its only sane answer.

To be honest, it was accidentally on purpose; I'd been campaigning against these units on the grounds they caused more risk than they saved, TB incidence having dropped considerably since their introduction. The mobile chest X-rays of the 1960s used a 35 millimetre camera looking at a fluoroscope screen which gave a very high exposure to X-rays. It was done to save the cost of large film. (See my 'Compulsory mass chest X-rays do more harm than good', Department of Clinical Science, J.C.S.M.R., ANU, 4 September 1974.)

What God or medicos do to us, doesn't count

When acceptable radiation levels are set for workers and the public, what radiates you naturally from outside and inside the body are discounted, and what medicos expose you to diagnostically is ignored.

The net biological effect of all sorts of radiation is homogenised in a single unit called a millisievert (mSv). Internationally the recommended level is 1 mSv of industry-related radiation exposure every year on top of what occurs 'naturally' because of environment or lifestyle. If you live close to sea level

Typical doses received during various diagnostic x-ray proceedures in Australia for 1996

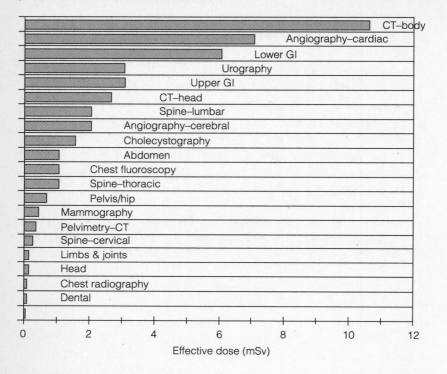

Effective dose (mSv)

in a typical, drafty Australian home, not set on mineral sands, then that 1 mSv per year is on top of an average of 1.5 mSv per year. The rest of the world gets a higher dose. In the United States, 5.8 million homes are above the action level for the natural radioactive gas radon in their homes which triggers at 5 mSv per year. As you can't sue God, nothing is done as a consequence. In Finland the average background level is 7 mSv per year. So in Australia we live with about 2.5 mSv per year; the Finns with about 8.5 mSv per year.

Because medicos always carefully weigh up the pros and cons of X-rays and discuss these with you (never saying, for example, 'let's take another one, just to be sure'), the 3 to 75 mSv for a body CAT scan, for example, never gets factored into recommended exposure levels.

A detailed analysis of radiation exposure, including medical, is given in 'Background Radiation Levels and Medical Exposure Levels in Australia, *Bulletin of the Australian Radiation Protection*

Society, 16 March 1999, pp. 7–14. It was (once) found on the web at address http://www.health.gov.au:80/arpansa/

In the course of a year we could clock up our 2.5 mSv dose pretty easily. We could travel by plane 10 kilometres up in the air (the aircrew have occupational exposure limits), or visit Jenolan Caves or Buchan Caves (the guides wear monitors), sit close to some glazed garden pots, lug a bag of soluble potash (potassium sulfate) or superphosphate around the garden (the United States used to get its uranium from Florida phosphate rock), visit a nuclear power station or waste reprocessing plant overseas, go skiing, wander continously outside Kakadu's uranium mines, and so on.

Countries with multiple industrial activities that can increase public exposure to radiation (such as nuclear power stations, mines—including coal mines, uranium reprocessing or weapons plants) often set dose constraints (in fractions of a millisievert) for each individual activity so that when added up, the total public exposure of the most exposed public is kept below an additional 1 mSv per year.

Internationally the occupational maximum allowance for workers in any industry (again on top of whatever is the local background) is 20 mSv per year. In practice levels of 6 mSV per year are rarely exceeded in Australia. The argument is that workers receive a benefit (salary) from the extra exposure.

With such an enormous spread in radiation exposure (natural and occupational) you would think that the hoary old argument relating radiation dose and radiation-induced cancers would be resolved. The Finns should be showing 3.5 times our rate.

Well, it seems it is still OK to live in Finland. Cancer rates do not correlate with the dose at their levels (8.5 mSv/year). But try to avoid areas with more than four times that exposure. That is beginning to get too high. So aren't we in the 'no worries' country?

I guess medicos (like Helen Caldicott) are attracted to anti-nuclear causes out of sheer guilty conscience! Let their irradiation of us be counted! Maybe 25 years on, the departments of health will again see some logic.

We rightly worry about the safety of our homes and of our families living in them. One of the most remarkable and cost-effective security devices is the domestic ceiling smoke-detector.

Home reactor

A delightful story is reported in the 'Reader's Digest' of David, an enterprising US student who one day decided he wanted to make a neutron gun. In 1994 the worldwide web was not as widely used but there were plenty of friendly scientists around with helpful hints. Be patriotic he was told; use americium.

Typically, less than 0.2 milligrams of americium 241 dioxide is used in a smoke detector. David used the inserts of 100 broken smoke detectors inside a hollow lead block with a small exit hole covered with aluminium foil. What to do with his device? How about a nuclear reactor? Fissile-enriched uranium 235 is a bit hard to come by, but no worries, the mantle in gas lanterns is (still often) coated with thorium 232 oxide to make it incandescent. Bombard these mantles with neutrons and produce uranium 233 which is also fissile. (In fact if or when we run out of uranium, thorium would be the next fuel.) A little chemical ingenuity was needed to extract and concentrate the thorium. It required buying lithium batteries and mixing lithium with the mantle ash and wrapping it in aluminium foil before heating.

Sadly, the neutron gun was not powerful enough for a chain reaction, so he was advised to replace the americium with radium. Radium is still widely available in the painted luminous dials of clocks of the 1950s. Scraping off paint is boring, and so he was lucky to find an original vial of radium paint. And a chemistry student told him that berylium is a much better alpha target for producing neutrons than is aluminium (and gave him a small strip). With a few trimmings (like slowing the neutrons down), his new package did produce lots of neutrons.

Now wildly ambitious, he decided to make a sort of breeder reactor, which would produce more radioactive fuel than it consumed. He succeeded only too well. But then he panicked, and so the US Feds were called and moved in with moonsuits.

There goes the neighbourhood. A contaminated 39 barrels of it were trucked off to a radioactive waste repository in the great Salt Lake Desert. And David has joined the US Navy.

For less than $10 we have purchased a sentinel ready to squawk loudly in warning if approached by smoke or steam. On the grounds of prudence and commonsense alone, the smoke detector is well nigh unassailable. But would you be so keen to bring extra radioactivity into your home? And what happens when the smoke detector and the extra radioactivity are one and the same?

The core of the smoke detector is actually a tiny piece of synthetic radioactive element—americium 241. It was made in a nuclear reactor from plutonium which was, in turn, made in a nuclear reactor from uranium. The radiation ionises the surrounding air and allows it to conduct electricity, sounding an alarm when smoke interferes with this process.

The smoke detector is a microcosm of the nuclear debate. It is clear that the safety benefits offered by the smoke detector far outweigh any risk to health. Smoke detectors are perfectly safe, while the americium 241 is fully enclosed within its own unit on the ceiling. It's what happens after the smoke detector has outlived its useful life (about 10 years) which really counts. With a half life of 430 years, the unit must—as required on the label—be returned to State Health authorities, then recycled or stored out of harm's way for a few thousand years.

The humble smoke detector is not a lone case. In 1999 some 8000 older style ZE 22/3 electricity meters were replaced in New South Wales with a more efficient model. The meters all contained a hot water control relay which used radium or tritium as an ionising aid. Again perfectly safe in place, but requiring careful disposal. Wrongful disposal of these sort of meters recently set off a Geiger counter at a Queensland tip.

The accident at Tokai fuel processing plant in October 1999 was rated four on a sort of Richter scale by the Japanese Government. The Chernobyl accident in 1986 scored seven on this scale. Tokai was more than an 'incident', and could be described as causing 'acute health effects to workers' as well as some public radiation exposure at about prescribed limits, but 'without significant off-site risk'. This puts it behind Three Mile Island (1979) rated 5, though that accident was less significant in its actual radiation effects (that is, the problem area was shielded from staff and others).

Criticality accidents have occurred before, all but two including Chernobyl prior to the early 1980s. Of the previous accidents, 37 occurred in connection with research reactors or military work, resulting in ten deaths. Another 22 occurred in fuel cycle facilities, resulting in seven deaths. They were almost entirely in the wet chemistry processes, due to putting too much uranium-bearing solution in one tank. Mostly the solutions then erupt rather like a saucepan of milk boiling over, and the fission reaction ceases as the material is ejected and dispersed in the immediate vicinity. None of the previous accidents resulted in significant release of radioactivity outside the plants. Practically all were in Russian or US plants. (More technical details can be found in www.uic.com.au)

Like in all applications of science and technology, gung-ho attitudes and careless behaviour can be dangerous and fatal. But nothing when compared to earthquakes, floods and fires.

What about the radioactive tailings from mining uranium?

Tailings are depleted ore with less radioactivity, but because of their fine grains they release more radon. They must be buried securely. For a real comparison, consider the same radio-active wastes from natural gas and oil production and refining. Like uranium mine tailings, these sludges contain radium residues. At drill sites they are buried, in refineries they are removed by regular descaling of heavily caked production pipes. Security of disposal of these wastes is nowhere near as stringent as for mining, and they are generally buried on site.

Fossil fuel supporters should not forget that (Australian) coal contains about 0.4 to 4 parts per million of uranium along with many other heavy metals; overseas it can be higher. Flyash left over from burning coal is more radioactive than the coal from which it is produced, but that does not mean it is hazardous. 'It may be advisable, however, to check the radioactivity of flyash to be used commercially, for example, as a partial replacement for cement in concrete.' (D. Swaine, 'Trace Elements in Coal—why the interest?', *Australian Coal Journal*, No. 34, 1991, p. 10.)

Then there is greenhouse. Every kilowatt hour of electricity in coal-burning Australia results in about 1 kilogram of carbon dioxide, adding up to 160 million tonnes per year, and much more is caused by our exports. Conversely, our uranium exports save 300 million tonnes of overseas-produced carbon dioxide. A number of European countries are ambivalent about nuclear power but they then import electricity from the 60 nuclear power stations in France which produce 76 per cent of French electricity.

Natural gas is better for greenhouse emissions than coal but not much. Which leaves solar and energy conservation initiatives the only long-term answer. The sooner the appropriate level of investment is made, the better.

Today's Information Age depends entirely on chips containing millions of transistors. Transistors are made from highly zone-refined silicon. For high quality applications, the first stage in chemical doping needed to make n-type conducting silicon is carried out in a nuclear reactor. Neutron irradiation of slabs of pure silicon turns around one in a billion silicon atoms uniformly throughout the slab into an atom phosphorus producing n-type semiconductor. Australia's ANSTO reactor has 15 per cent of the world market for this. While currently too expensive for everyday devices, one day your computer, mobile phone, TV, CD and everything else electronic will be totally dependent on neutron irradiation in nuclear reactors. Just think of that.